CW00554754

Big Questions in an Age
of Global Crises

Big Questions in an Age of Global Crises

Thinking about Meaning, Purpose,
God, Suffering, Death, and Living Well
during Pandemics, Wars, Economic
Collapse, and Other Disasters

Nick Megoran

Foreword by Sharon Dirckx

WIPF & STOCK · Eugene, Oregon

BIG QUESTIONS IN AN AGE OF GLOBAL CRISES
Thinking about Meaning, Purpose, God, Suffering, Death, and Living Well
during Pandemics, Wars, Economic Collapse, and Other Disasters

Copyright © 2022 Nick Megoran. All rights reserved. Except for brief
quotations in critical publications or reviews, no part of this book may
be reproduced in any manner without prior written permission from the
publisher. Write: Permissions, Wipf and Stock Publishers, 199 W. 8th Ave.,
Suite 3, Eugene, OR 97401.

Wipf & Stock
An Imprint of Wipf and Stock Publishers
199 W. 8th Ave., Suite 3
Eugene, OR 97401

www.wipfandstock.com

PAPERBACK ISBN: 978-1-6667-3510-9
HARDCOVER ISBN: 978-1-6667-9184-6
EBOOK ISBN: 978-1-6667-9185-3

06/20/22

Unless otherwise indicated, scriptures taken from the Holy Bible, New International Version®, NIV®. Copyright © 1973, 1978, 1984, 2011 by Biblica,
Inc.™ Used by permission of Zondervan. All rights reserved worldwide.
www.zondervan.com The "NIV" and "New International Version" are
trademarks registered in the United States Patent and Trademark Office by
Biblica, Inc.™

Dedicated to the members of Wallsend Baptist Church
and to the geography students of Newcastle University,
who are not afraid to ask the big questions.

Contents

Foreword

WE ASK QUESTIONS ALL the time. Some belong firmly in the everyday category, such as questions around what to eat and drink, how to spend our free time, and which Netflix series to watch. Others have rather more significance, such as questions around if and whom to marry, where to live, and what kind of career to pursue. Still others are potential game-changers, such as questions around whether or not this life has any ultimate meaning, whether or not God exists, and what happens when we die.

This third category of questions has been harder to ignore in the wake of the COVID-19 pandemic. After all, the spread of a deadly virus across the world has reminded us of two things. First, life is fragile and can deteriorate and end in a matter of days or hours. Second, we are deeply relational beings who are not meant to be on our own and isolated from others. Questions about life and its ultimate purpose have become front and center once again.

Where do we go with our questions?

Should we squash them or address them?

Are there any helpful answers?

If you have been asking questions, no matter the size, then you will find this engaging and clearly written book extremely helpful. Nick Megoran, whom I have known for over two decades since his days as a PhD student in Cambridge, is an author who takes your questions seriously. In this book, *Big Questions in an Age of Global Crises,* he will help you to unpack your questions and will show how Christian thinking offers some compelling insights that are worth grappling with.

Nick does not presume his readers to hold Christian belief, though he will seek to persuade you that it's actually *if God exists* that we are able to make best sense of why deep questions arise in the first place. A common misunderstanding about Christian belief is that it carries us off into a fairy tale world that has no bearing on the gritty reality that we happen to live in. Yet, the opposite is true. Christianity stands or falls on historic events. Jesus Christ died a gruesome death under the rule of Roman Emperor Caesar Augustus in AD 34. The question is: Did he rise again three days later? If so, this could not be more relevant to us all, as we ponder matters of life and death amid a global pandemic. Nick is also candid about his own journey from unbelief to faith in Jesus Christ as a young adult, and the difference it made in life. He invites you into his own story and shares the stories of many others as you journey through this book.

This is far from the first writing of this kind for Nick. He is the author of several other books, including *Warlike Christians in an Age of Violence* (Wipf & Stock, 2017), and has also written for *The Guardian* (2019). Further, as an established academic and professor of political geography, Nick has written widely and with clarity and influence. But he is no ivory-tower thinker. Even his work as an academic geographer has focused on the impact of political realities on peoples' lives, and in particular in Central Asia.

But add to this that Nick is also the pastor of a church in Wallsend, Tyneside, and the responses offered here in this book have been honed and borne out in the experience of leading people through a time of national crisis. On such big topics it is not possible to offer comprehensive responses, but nor will you find trite ones. Nick is grounded and practical and writes with the mind of an academic, the compassion of a husband and father, and the heart of a pastor, with a decent dose of humor thrown in.

If you have big questions, do not ignore them. Keep reading. It may be the most important thing you do this year.

Sharon Dirckx
Speaker and Author,
OCCA The Oxford Centre
for Christian Apologetics

Introduction

Big Questions during Turbulent Times

WHAT BIG QUESTIONS ABOUT life have you faced at times of personal, national, or global crisis?

In April 2020, an article for the UK's ITV media outlet said that "the coronavirus lockdown in the UK has raised a lot of questions,"[1] and identified the ten most Googled coronavirus searches. They fell into two main sorts. The first were medical and epidemiological, like "How to know if you have coronavirus," and "How to treat coronavirus." The second type were about practical responses, such as "How to claim benefits during coronavirus" and "How to make face masks for coronavirus."

These are important and useful things to know, but there is a third set of more profound questions raised by crises like the COVID-19 pandemic that people have been asking but would be unlikely to put to Google. Is there any meaning, purpose, and value to my life? How do I face death and what happens after I die? Does God exist? If so, how could he allow suffering like this terrible virus? And how can I live life well during these traumatic times? Humans have always asked such big questions, but a time of crisis like a pandemic, war or a terror attack, genocide, or economic or

1. ITV, "Life in Lockdown," para. 1.

political collapse pushes them to the front of our minds and makes them harder to ignore. The purpose of this book is to help you think them through.

Although this book is about some fundamental philosophical and religious questions, it is written primarily from a practical rather than a theoretical perspective. This is because of the two jobs that I, the author, have. First, as a university professor of political geography, I am used to conducting fieldwork and interviewing people across the world. In this book you will encounter some of the people I have met and places I have visited in my research on war, nationalist conflict, and economic crises. You will also come across examples of real and imaginary people from films, novels, biographies, and music whose stories help us think through the weighty issues under discussion in an engaging way. Second, as a pastor of a church during the COVID-19 pandemic I was daily reminded of the everyday importance of making sense of, and responding well to, what was happening. This book is therefore illustrated throughout with practical examples of how Christian people, today and in previous ages, have responded to crises, including pandemics, terrorism and war, industrial disasters, and tyrannical rule.

It is written from a Christian perspective. This is because in my twenties I wrestled with questions like these myself and, having considered different worldviews, eventually found in the Bible the most satisfying and convincing answers that made the best sense of the world around me. Some of that story is shared in the book. But it is not written assuming that the reader shares a belief in the Christian faith or the reliability of the Bible. Nor could such a short book claim to be a comprehensive or exhaustive study of the weighty issues under discussion. Rather, it attempts the more modest goal of persuading the reader that Christian thinking offers some reasonable and practical insights and answers to these big questions, answers that are worth spending some time considering.

Although chapter 5 has its origins in a public lecture at Newcastle University, this book began life as an online discussion group that began in April 2020 out of Wallsend Baptist Church as the UK locked down under the shadow of the coronavirus pandemic. I am grateful to Donna Mear and Scott Kirkley for helping me run it, and to everyone who took part in the discussions. The active participation of students and townsfolk, young and old, and Christians and sceptics, helped both refine my thinking and persuade me that the arguments and discussions developed there might be of interest to a wider audience in the form of this book. Facing big questions about life, God, and the universe is an unavoidable part of what makes us human, and I hope that this book helps you as you grapple with them.

1

Does Life Have Meaning, Purpose, and Value?

OVER NINE SUCCESSIVE DAYS in 1945, Holocaust survivor and Austrian Jewish psychologist Viktor Frankl wrote what has been hailed as one of the twentieth century's most impressive books on living life well, *Man's Search For Meaning*. Reflecting on his own observations and experiences, he set out to understand how people managed to survive the horrors of Auschwitz and the other Nazi death camps that he himself had endured. He concluded that the key factor was neither physical strength nor intelligence, as we might have expected, but rather whether people could find *meaning* in life. This might come from different sources such as memories of cherished loved ones, a determination to complete a book or piece of music, or a belief that suffering had some purpose. Quoting the German philosopher Friedrich Nietzsche, he argued that "He who has a *why* to live for can bear with almost any *how*."[1] By the time Frankl died in 1997 the book had sold more than 10 million copies and been translated into 24 languages.[2] This surprised Frankl,

1. Kushner, "Preface," 7 (emphasis mine).
2. Noble, "Dr. Viktor E. Frankl of Vienna," para. 7.

who said that when he had written it he was thinking that perhaps it might speak helpfully to a smaller number of people suffering from severe depression. He commented in the preface to the 1992 edition that if so many people "reach out for a book whose very title promises to deal with the question of a meaning to life, it must be a question that burns under their fingernails."[3]

As COVID-19 pandemic lockdowns took effect across the world in March 2020, most people had to find new ways to entertain themselves. One of my distractions was rearing butterflies and moths. In April some puss moths, *Cerura vinula*, that I had bred the previous year as caterpillars hatched from the cocoons in which they had overwintered. Looking excitedly at these beautiful creatures, my daughter asked what they do. I replied, only one thing—reproduce. They have no mouths so they don't need to eat, and their only purpose or activity in the few days in which they live is to avoid predators long enough to find a mate and lay eggs. Then they die, shortly afterwards tiny caterpillars emerge from the eggs, and it all starts over again. My daughter retorted, "That's pointless!"

It might seem that way to us, but does a puss moth worry whether its life is "pointless?" I suspect not. But we humans do. We all want life to have some purpose or meaning, and we want to feel that our lives are valuable. We see this in the autobiographies of the rich and famous. When I was a teenager my favorite music group was Queen. I used to shut my bedroom door tight, play their cassettes at a loud volume, hold a bottle of deodorant in front of my mouth as though it were a microphone, and sing along, pretending that I was on stage! It was the closest I ever got to being a rock star. But perhaps I wouldn't have wanted to be one. Queen's lead singer, Freddie Mercury, said in a 1985 interview, "You can have everything in the world and still be the loneliest man, and that is the most bitter type of loneliness."[4] Success, he said, had brought him "world idolisation and millions of pounds," but prevented him "from having the one thing we all need" for a fulfilling and meaningful human life—"a loving, on-going relationship." In the same

3. Frankl, *Man's Search for Meaning*, 11.
4. Feinstein, "Rock On, Freddie," para. 4.

decade, the *Carry On* series of comedy films was a staple of British television. Kenneth Williams, with his unique nasal voice, was one of the funniest actors on set. Yet he wrote in his autobiography: "I wonder if anyone will ever stand in a room that I have lived in and touch the things that were once a part of my life . . . [and] will ever know about the emptiness of my life, and wonder about me?" The last entry in his diary was, "Oh what's the bloody point?"[5]

Lucy Kellaway was an "agony aunt" on London's *Financial Times* newspaper, responding to the personal worries and concerns of the country's financial elites who wrote to her. She observed:

> We are in the middle of an epidemic of meaningless-
> ness at work. Bankers, lawyers, and senior managers are
> increasingly asking themselves what on earth their jobs
> mean, and finding it hard to come up with an answer . . .
> I get asked all the time by successful professionals—what
> is it all about?[6]

I suppose that most of us share, at some point, those feelings of being empty or lost, of questioning where our lives are heading and whether everything that we do really has any point. Such feelings can become more acute at times of crisis in our individual or collective lives. When faced with fear, bereavement, unemployment, uncertainty, and isolation, the questions of whether our lives have meaning, purpose, and value become acute. This is particularly the case when we can't do the things that gave them meaning before, such as work or being with loved ones.

We often try and push away those nagging questions about meaning. A friend said to me, as the COVID-19 pandemic swept aside normal life, "My strategy to keep my sanity in these strange times is to not think of the big questions at all, the biggest question I can handle without increasing my anxiety these days is: What is for lunch?!" That is understandable, especially when shopping for basic goods in empty supermarket aisles was so hard. But these questions never completely go away, they haunt us until we die.

5. Barnes, "Who Killed Kenneth Williams?," para. 6.
6. Kellaway, "Point of View."

"Man's [or humanity's] search for meaning," as Viktor Frankl put it, is simply not one that we can avoid. In this chapter I suggest that life really does have meaning, purpose, and value, but that we can't know what they are without reference to the God who made us.

The Universal Search for God

As a young man, my father-in-law used to race pigeons. He and others in his club in the eastern English county of Norfolk would tag their prize birds, and put them together in a special crate which was packed on a train and sent on a 250-mile journey to the northern town of Morpeth. The railway staff would open the crate and the birds would fly home, the first one back winning the race. We can think of our search for meaning as being like a homing instinct drawing us back to our maker.

Ernest Becker, in his Pulitzer-Prize winning book *The Denial of Death*, argues that much of modern civiliation is about trying to avoid those haunting questions of meaning and purpose. "Modern man is drinking and drugging himself out of awareness, or he spends his time shopping, which is the same thing," he writes.[7] We pile up money in the bank, try to advance our careers and enjoy life through leisure, seek a bigger home or the best car in the neighbourhood, but underneath, he continues, still "throbs the ache of cosmic specialness." The longing for meaning is everywhere, Becker argues, and the ways we avoid it can be extremely damaging.

I suspect that deep down we all know Becker is right. We try to ignore the nagging questions about whether what we are doing and how we are living has any purpose, filling up the emptiness by doing things, achieving things, buying things, imbibing things, and through relationships. But that throbbing "ache of cosmic specialiness" won't go away. We are not satisfied with simply eating and drinking and finding shelter and provision, and with sex and procreation. We yearn for more. We are not puss moths!

---

7. Becker, *Denial of Death*, 284.

Does Life Have Meaning, Purpose, and Value?

Sometimes those questions fall silent, sometimes they nag in the background, but at other times they assail us. I would like to use my own experiences to illustrate this. I went to sleep on January 3rd, 1995, happy and content, thriving in my final year at university, supported by a caring family and good friends, and planning exciting future travel and a career when my studies came to an end that summer. I woke up at 8am on January 4th with an inexplicable, overwhelming feeling that my world had fallen apart. I still find it hard to describe, but it was as if an enormous and terrifying void had opened up inside me, and darkness was all around. I was besieged with questions I had never really thought about before. Does life have meaning? Can we know truth? Is there a God? Is there any value to what I am doing? What happens when I die? There was no obvious reason for this change.

The next two and a half years were the hardest of my life, as I wrestled daily with these questions. During this period I lived in many different places and amongst a wide variety of people, and what struck me most of all was that wherever I went people were trying to give meaning to their lives. I spent half a year surviving on unemployment benefits in one of the UK's most deprived neighbourhoods, Tottenham, in London, reading philosophy books all day long in a local university library as I tried (but failed) to find a job. I started at the ancient Greeks and worked forwards, and each evening I read poetry books from the local municipal library. All this thought, art, and culture was directly asking about our purpose. It was clear to me that I was far from the first person to be troubled this way—this search for meaning goes back at least to the dawn of written history. While in London I hung out with peace activists and remember going to a demonstration against a weapons trade fair. The young woman next to me was screaming in fury at people driving in past the line of police. As we spoke she told me that she felt lost and empty in life, but going from demonstration to demonstration, shouting at the people she regarded as the bad guys, and thinking that she was working for justice and peace with a community of like-minded people helped her feel that she was doing something valuable, briefly numbing the pain of life.

After six months I left Tottenham to live with a traditional farming family in a beautiful valley in the mountains of Central Asia. As I sunk into their seasonal rhythms, I saw how social norms and expectations gave meaning in a very hierarchical society. Young people were at the bottom of the pile, but as they married and had children, and took on responsible roles as good members of the neighborhood and society, they gained respect and a sense that their lives had meaning. I also spent time living in a big nearby city, and one of my friends there suddenly hit the big time in his business career. He used his newfound wealth to throw himself into a hedonistic life of parties and pleasure, until he lost it all after being cheated in a reckless venture and ended up in a mental asylum as the meaning he had built in his life upon crashed down around him. At the same time, I associated with religious people in mosques and churches, listening to teaching by mullahs and pastors, and saw how the practice of their faiths helped them calibrate their lives as meaningful and valuable. This period was bookended by time at Durham and Cambridge universities as I completed my undergraduate studies and began a PhD. I noticed how academics researched, wrote, and presented their ideas in articles and to each other, and in so doing created communities that affirmed to each other that what they were doing was meaningful and valuable even though, as my nonuniversity friend Barry put it, to outsiders it all looked "trivial."

What struck me most was that all these very different people in all their various ways were essentially doing the same thing—searching for meaning and value and creating communities of people and activities that helped generate and ascribe meaning and value to their lives. No other animal, we can assume, is so troubled by these questions. This puzzled me—why should this be so? Why couldn't we just be happy with simply feeding our natural appetites by eating, drinking, keeping safe and warm, and reproducing, like any other animal? We wouldn't expect this yearning for meaning in a universe described by atheists, where life was a random and meaningless accident. But we would expect that in a world made by God and populated by people in whom he has set an intrinsic orientation towards him.

At that time I read the book of Ecclesiastes in the Bible, which is a collection of philosophical musings attributed to King Solomon. I was struck by one phrase, that humanity searches for meaning and happiness because God "has put eternity in their hearts."[8] The most rational explanation of all I had observed seemed to me that we were made that way. I came to decide, somewhat reluctantly, that the most reasonable and rational way to make sense of all this was to conclude that the search for meaning was like my father-in-law's homing pigeons, a hard-wired instinct calling us back to our creator. Or as Saint Augustine, another philosopher I read while in Tottenham, put it of his quest for meaning, "You have made us for yourself and our hearts are restless until they find their rest in you."[9] The universality of the search for meaning suggests it is not something that is culturally specific, but rather has been deeply placed within us. C. S. Lewis suggests that "God makes no appetite in vain"[10]—we yearn for meaning because we have been made by a God who placed that yearning in us, a God who wants us to satisfy it in him.

We Can't Know That Meaning without God

The search for meaning is everywhere, I have argued—but it can be very dangerous. As a lecturer in political geography, I have researched nationalism and its oftentimes deadly effects all around the world. Among the best books ever written on the topic is veteran *New York Times* foreign correspondent Chris Hedges's *War Is a Force That Gives Us Meaning*. He records how the "plague of nationalism" can overtake apparently reasonable people with astonishing speed as war erupts. From war zones across the world,

8. Eccl 3:11.

9. Augustine, *Confessions*, 3, lines 8–9.

10. Lewis, "Learning in War-Time," 33.

he provides grim, eyewitness accounts of how he has seen people excuse and even revel in horrible injustices and cruelties as they identified with "their" side. "The enduring attraction of war," he argues, is that it can give us what we long for in life. It can give us purpose, reason, a meaning for living." He concludes that "Many of us, restless and unfulfilled, see no supreme worth in our lives. We want more out of life. And war, at least, gives us a sense that we can rise above our smallness."[11]

I argued above that humanity's near-universal search for meaning is best understood as a clue pointing us to God. But because some of the different meanings people find in life can be very destructive to themselves or others, we need a way to judge between meanings. I want to suggest, secondly, that without God there is no way to judge between these meanings.

For example, take two different interpretations of the meaning of life. Michael Shermer, founder of *Skeptic Magazine*, said this:

> Play hard, work hard, love hard. . . . The bottom line for me is to live life to the fullest in the here-and-now instead of a hoped-for hereafter, and make every day count in some meaningful way and do something—no matter how small it is—to make the world a better place.[12]

In contrast, Mongolian chroniclers record that Genghis (Chinggis) Khan, one of the most successful political leaders of all time who built history's largest contiguous land empire by pillaging his way across Asia and into Europe in the thirteenth century, is reputed to have said that:

> the greatest happiness is to vanquish your enemies, to chase them before you, to rob them of their wealth, to see those dear to them bathed in tears, to clasp to your bosom their wives and daughters.[13]

---

11. Hedges, *War Is a Force*, 3–7.
12. Shermer, "Bottom Line."
13. Albeity, "Capturing Chinggis Qahan," para. 11.

For Shermer, the meaning of play hard, work hard, love hard is to make the world better; for Khan, it is, literally, pillage and murder and rape. How do you judge between them?

If the universe is meaningless, if atheism is right and there is no author to our story, then we can't appeal upwards to a higher authority (God) and so there is no way of saying authoritatively which is the true meaning. We can then do one of three things. We can say that everyone's interpretation of a meaningful life is equally valid—but that would mean that Khan's pillage and murder was on an equal footing to Shermer's making the world a better place, something we would shrink back from as intolerable. Second, we can try to smuggle in values by the back door, saying things like "everyone knows murder is wrong." But if we have no absolute way of judging, then that's simply relying on someone else's value system, all the while pretending that we aren't. It is intellectually lazy and dishonest, and it wouldn't allow us to answer Khan. The third option is to fight it out, seeing who has the power to impose their definition of acceptable meaning on others. But in a two-way contest between Genghis Khan and Michael Shermer, my money would be on Khan!

But what if there *is* an author? American novelist Kurt Vonnegut wrote an intriguing book called *Breakfast of Champions*.[14] Imagine that you and I are sitting in a bus next to each other discussing it. I say, "The title's real meaning is *Breakfast of Champignons*. It is about French cuisine, and the best ways to find and cook wild mushrooms for your early morning meal." "No," you reply, "that's nonsense. It is really about the high-protein diets of Olympic swimmers"—and you remind me that swimmer Michael Phelps, one of greatest Olympic athletes ever, used to eat for breakfast three fried egg sandwiches, three chocolate chip pancakes, a five-egg omelette, and three sugar-coated slices of eggy bread, all washed down with two cups of coffee.[15]

Imagine that we are arguing away about this, getting louder and more impassioned, when someone taps us on the shoulder

14. Vonnegut, *Breakfast of Champions*.
15. "Food for Fuel."

and we look round to see that Kurt Vonnegut himself is sitting behind us on the bus. He asks what we are doing, and we tell him we are arguing about whether *Breakfast of Champions* is about French foraging cuisine or elite athletes' diets. He would say, "No, you are both wrong. I am the author of the book, and I can tell you its meaning: it is a novel about a character called Kilgore Trout travelling to a ceremony to collect a publishing prize."[16]

In the Bible, the apostle Peter describes Jesus Christ as "the author of life,"[17] that is, the author of our story who can explain what its meaning is. This does not mean a distant creator who stands outside his story. My favorite scene in Vonnegut's novel is when Kilgore Trout is sitting at a bar, and suddenly a strange feeling comes over him. He turns, and sees that the reason is that Kurt Vonnegut himself—his author and creator—has entered the room. The author has written himself into the story! Likewise, the Bible says that in Jesus Christ, God has himself entered our world, lived amongst us, and showed us what life's purpose is—to be in a loving relationship with God: as he prayed, "Father, I want those you have given me to be with me."[18] To illustrate this, Jesus told a story about a wayward son who had insulted his father, took his share of the inheritance, and left home. After squandering it he was forced by starvation and desperation to sheepishly return, rehearsing his grovelling apology on the way back. But Jesus says, "while he was still a long way off, his father saw him and was filled with compassion for him; he ran to his son, threw his arms around him, and kissed him."[19] As Daniel Clark comments on this, relating back to Freddie Mercury's desperate plea, "What better 'loving, ongoing relationship' could we want?"[20]

---

16. Although he uses a different example, this illustration is inspired by Bannister, *The Atheist Who Didn't Exist*, 174.

17. Acts 3:15

18. John 17:24.

19. Luke 15:20.

20. Clark, *Dead or Alive?*, 64.

Human Value

I have argued that the universal search for meaning points us to God, and that we can't know that meaning without reference to God. This leads to a final and extremely important consideration: God's purposes for us—that we should love and know him—show that *humans have intrinsic value.*

That we need to feel valued is demonstrated by the story of Keira (not her real name). I met her when researching experiences of work after the 2007–08 financial crisis. Keira works in an industry that, under financial pressure in a more competitive market, has increasingly switched from using permanent members of staff to employing temporary ones. These staff are cheaper, as their wages are lower and they are entitled to fewer benefits. Although highly qualified, Keira was forced to undertake relatively menial tasks that helped her manager progress his career but impeded hers. She felt unvalued: this system made economic sense to her employer, but was "not conducive to me being a person," she told me. It amounted to "the systematic destruction of my self-esteem and dismissal of my personal ambitions. . . . There wasn't a single annual review that I didn't leave in tears." She used psychologist Martin Seligman's famous term "learned helplessness"[21] to describe her state, a condition that can be observed in laboratory rats and dogs when they are punished indiscriminately and end up docile and dulled. In short, Keira wasn't treated in a way that made her feel valuable.

But, we should ask, was Keira justified in feeling this? Is there any basis on which we can say humans *are* valuable and should be treated thus? In 2017, Newcastle University (where I work as a geography lecturer) unveiled a statue to mark a half century since Martin Luther King Jr. visited to receive an honorary degree. It is a fascinating story. At a time when he was furiously busy back home, he and his aide, Andrew Jackson, made a grueling visit by plane and night train to spend only a few hours in a recently established provincial university. His 1967 visit was all but forgotten until the

21. Seligman, "Learned Helplessness."

1990s when Brian Ward, a young history lecturer, uncovered the lost film of the ceremony and the moving impromptu acceptance speech he delivered. In the speech King identified the "three urgent and indeed great problems" that pervade our world "as racism, poverty, and war." Watching the film today is poignant as it proved to be his last trip outside of the Americas before his murder in April 1968.[22]

Although hated and feared by many Americans in his own time, King is now widely regarded as a great moral leader, and unveiling the statue caught the imagination of national and international media. But *why* did King devote his life to opposing racism, poverty, and war? He did not do so because that's what civilized, cultured, decent people do. History shows that wars are usually started by such people, who often benefit from racism and wealth inequalities. Rather, he was driven by the belief that people were made, as the Bible puts it, "in the image of God,"[23] and that this had significant moral implications. As he said in 1965, racial segregation was wrong first and foremost because we are made in God's image: "The innate worth referred to in the phrase the image of God is universally shared in equal portions by all . . . Every man must be respected because God loves him."[24] In contrast to the view of many white Southerners at the time who saw African-Americans primarily as laborers, King insisted that "man is not a thing. He must be dealt with not as an 'animated tool,' but as a person sacred in himself. To do otherwise is to depersonalize the potential person and desecrate what he is."[25]

These are stirring words, but if atheism is correct, and if it is pushed to its logical conclusions, then Martin Luther King Jr. was totally and profoundly deluded. According to this worldview, human beings are not sacred creatures, made in the image of God. They are not bearers of intrinsic rights and dignity. They are merely an accident of time, evolution, and chance, and there

22. Ward, *Martin Luther King in Newcastle upon Tyne*, 68.
23. Gen 1:27.
24. King, "Martin Luther King Jr. Speech," 118.
25. King, "Martin Luther King Jr. Speech," 118.

is no fundamental reason why we shouldn't treat them exactly as Genghis Khan did.

I once took part in a public debate on this topic with an atheist, and at one point he said, "Oh, I wish you'd stop going on about Genghis Khan, that was a long time ago and we're more civilised now." I replied that the millions of people who have died in recent conflicts in the former Yugoslavia, the Democratic Republic of Congo, Syria, Iraq, and a host of other places, are evidence that, unfortunately, this isn't true. But an example from modern Western societies about how we treat the weak in care institutions brings the point close to home.

In Britain, a disturbing proportion of people who died in the early months of the COVID-19 pandemic died in care homes. The condition and regulation of these institutions had been neglected for many years, and the welfare of their residents was not prioritized in initial emergency measures that the government took. It is difficult to escape the conclusion that society chose to regard those weak, frail lives as of less value. In a fascinating book the atheist philosopher Raimond Gaita describes a job he had as a seventeen-year-old working in a psychiatric hospital. It was a grim Victorian building surrounded by an iron fence, graveled but with no grass. Some patients had been there for decades. When they soiled themselves, as they often did, they were told to step into a shower, undress, and clean themselves: they were then mopped down from the distance of a mop-handle, the way zoo-keepers clean elephants.

"The patients were judged to be incurable and they appeared to have irretrievably lost everything which gives meaning to our lives," he said. "There were no grounds for self-respect, self-esteem, nothing we could congratulate them on; they had no visits from friends, wives, parents, or children. Most doctors and nurses looked down on them."

He recounts that one day a nun came to work on the ward. She made a huge impression: from her demeanor, to the way she spoke and her facial expressions, she showed up everyone else on staff. He was stunned at what he called "the quality of her love." She treated the patients with the dignity that other staff had ceased to afford them. She did this because she believed that they were God's children and equally loved and valued by him.

Gaita was deeply impressed. Yet as an atheist he said this: "We may say that all human beings are inestimably precious, that they are ends in themselves, that they are owed unconditional respect, that they possesses inalienable rights, and, of course, that they possess inalienable dignity." But he concludes, perhaps wistfully, "In my judgment these are ways of saying what we feel we need to say" and an atheist cannot really say them.[26]

Gaita is right: if there is no God, then human life can have no intrinsic value—with terrible consequences in the real world. That is because there is then no reason not to treat them just as birds and bats treat puss moths: valuable only as prey, to be gobbled down without any qualms. From care homes to killing fields to the way people like Keira are treated as disposable "human resources" in the workplace, we see the implications of this everywhere. In contrast, the Bible's teaching is that we are made in God's image, made to love and know him, and that each of us matters intrinsically—and this should be reflected in the way that we in turn treat other people. Life *does* have meaning and purpose and value. The big questions we find ourselves asking at times of crisis *do* matter, and the answers that we reach as individuals and societies matter profoundly in the real world.

More than just Moths

Anna Nobili had a difficult childhood growing up in the Italian city of Milan. Her family was poor and her parents separated when she was young, and when she needed money she took a job in a bar. She became an erotic dancer in a nightclub, enticing men in by acting as a target for their sexual conquest. She later said in an interview, "I was wasting my life dancing for men in clubs. The nights were filled with sex and alcohol. It was an empty life but

26. Gaita, *Common Humanity*, 17–24.

I liked it because I was the centre of attention."[27] One night her mother came into her room when she was getting ready to go to a nightclub and asked her to come to church with her instead. Anna felt an almost violent reaction against her—she regarded church as just for old people.

However, one Christmas Eve, for no reason she can give, she did go to midnight mass. She felt very moved with the priest repeatedly telling the congregation that God loves them, the one thing she was desperate to hear. She started to search for God, going on a retreat at Assisi. Whilst there, she recounted, "I was struck by how beautiful the sky was. I saw something fluorescent within the clouds, a cascade of colour and I felt the presence of God, the Creator."[28] She became a nun, working for an order who have everyday jobs and salaries, but using her life story and dance to help young people discover the real meaning of life.

Anna's story reminds us that we are not puss moths. The nagging sense that we want our lives to have purpose and meaning and value are like the homing instinct in pigeons drawing us back to our Creator. We can try to ignore it, but it haunts us; we can try and fill it with something else, like Anna did, but that so easily turns destructive. Although my story is different from Anna's (for me, the thought of dancing every night is more like the threat of punishment than a drug!), I reached the same conclusion as she did. Through my own observations of how we thirst for meaning, and my studies of what happens when we find that meaning in things that are damaging and harmful, I became convinced that we can't know the authentic meaning, purpose, and value of our lives without reference to God, the Author of our lives who steps into our story and seeks relationship with us. This of course begs the question that we will consider in the next chapter: How can we know whether God exists?

27. "Ex-Lap Dancer Now 'Dances for God,'" para. 5.
28. Pisa, "Like a Prayer," paras. 13–14.

2

Can We Know Whether God Exists?

IN 1969, THE CULT BBC satirical comedy show *Monty Python's Flying Circus* included a sketch about a debate on the existence of God, called "The Epilogue: A Question of Belief." It began with the presenter introducing the two participants in his clipped BBC English accent. First, in the full robes of a cardinal, was Monsignor Edward Gay, Visiting Pastoral Emissary of the Somerset Theological College and author of a number of books about belief. Opposite him sat Dr. Tom Jack: humanist, broadcaster, lecturer, and author. The scene was set for a serious debate. However, the presenter continued, "Tonight, instead of discussing the existence or nonexistence of God, they have decided to fight for it. The existence, or nonexistence, to be determined by two falls, two submissions, or a knockout. All right boys, let's get to it."[1] The two participants stand up, disrobe, and thrash it out in the wrestling ring.

This classic sketch—and we'll come back to the result later on—says two things about the question, "Can we know whether God exists?" The first is that many people see it as a joke. In 2009, singer Regina Spektor released a striking track entitled "Laughing With." God can be funny or hilarious, the song observes, when

1. Chapman et al. *Monty Python's Flying Circus,* 24–25.

listening to a joke at party which likens him to Santa Claus. But the refrain insists that no one laughs at God in a war or in a hospital.

Global crises shows that she's right. In the days following the September 11th, 2001 terrorist attacks in the USA, the UK's BBC Radio 4 station halted its daily evening comedy shows. As the COVID-19 pandemic struck, suddenly our parties were brought to a grinding halt, and we were stalked by the shadows of fear, sickness, bereavement, and death. The news was dominated by the daily grim statistics of infection and death, and of harrowing stories of hospitals and care homes overwhelmed. "No one laughs at God in a hospital," especially during a pandemic, when the big questions of life seem more pressing and less easy to avoid.

But is this question about whether God exists actually answerable by reasoned reflection? The second implication of the *Monty Python* sketch is that it is beyond the realms of rational debate. This was a theme of popular early-twenty-first-century writers nicknamed the "New Atheists." In an interview for Salon.com about his best-selling book, *The God Delusion*, Richard Dawkins said:

> A delusion is something that people believe in despite a total lack of evidence. Religion is scarcely distinguishable from childhood delusions like the 'imaginary friend' and the bogeyman under the bed. Unfortunately the God delusion possesses adults, and not just a minority of unfortunates in an asylum.[2]

Dawkins goes on to claim that although there is "no evidence"[3] for God's existence, the question "cannot be settled by reasoned argument because reasoned argument is drummed out of those trained in religion from the cradle."[4] This is striking—essentially, Dawkins argues that *Monty Python* really was right all along.

Is Dawkins correct that the question of God's existence is beyond reasoned, evidential reflection? Previous generations of atheist thinkers would have disagreed as they sought to persuade

2. Slack, "Atheist," para. 26.
3. Slack, "Atheist," para. 19.
4. Slack, "Atheist," para. 28.

people of their beliefs, and it is worth observing that Dawkins's approach to religion and atheism is regarded somewhat disparagingly by many atheist philosophers who have a better grasp of the history of this debate and are more cautious in their claims. Similarly, from its earliest foundations Christianity believed it had a solid evidential basis on which it could convince people of its truth claims by submitting itself to rational scrutiny. The New Testament book The Acts of the Apostles depicts the apostle Paul traveling round the Mediterranean world reasoning, persuading, and debating with all manner of people as his chief strategy for establishing churches: "As was his custom, Paul went into the synagogue, and on three Sabbath days he reasoned with them from the Scriptures,"[5] it records of his visit to Thessalonica. I have known many people who believe in God who didn't used to, and others who no longer believe when they once did: and in all cases, people can articulate reasons for this (some better than others).

There are many good reasons that can be given for the existence of God. In an influential lecture philosopher Alvin Plantinga identified "Two Dozen (or so) Theistic Arguments" (that is, arguments for God's existence).[6] These are not incontrovertible proofs in the way that I can prove that one of my fingers is slightly longer than another: we don't usually have those for questions about God and justice and truth and meaning and love and beauty and all those other higher-order issues that matter so much to us. Rather, we can see these arguments as pointers or clues which have led me, and many others, to conclude that belief in God is more reasonable and rational than nonbelief. In this chapter I will briefly consider four of these clues: scientific evidence, anthropological (human) evidence, morality, and God's communication to us through the person of Jesus Christ.

5. Acts 17:2.

6. Walls and Dougherty, *Two Dozen (or so) Arguments for God.*

Scientific Evidence

The first clue to the existence of God is scientific evidence. Perhaps the greatest scientific advance in my lifetime has been the mapping of the human genome. Knowing the complete set of our DNA has allowed us to understand the cellular blueprint for building humans, and will have a major impact on the medical and life sciences going forward. In the year 2000, scientists and world leaders gathered in person at the White House and by livelink from across the globe for the formal ceremony to mark this. President Bill Clinton said, "we are learning the language in which God created life." The lead scientist on the project, Francis Collins, echoed this: "It's a happy day for the world. It is humbling for me, and awe-inspiring, to realize that we have caught the first glimpse of our own instruction book, previously known only to God."[7]

It might have surprised some people that God was so central to this event, but that is only because a false idea has emerged in pop culture (propagated most virulently by people like Richard Dawkins in the West, and by Communist propaganda in the former Soviet Union) that there is somehow an implacable war between science and religion. Historically, this is simply not true, and no reputable historian of science would agree with it. I did my PhD at Cambridge University and used to regularly cycle past the old Cavendish laboratory. This is one of the most important institutions in the emergence of modern science, where the structure of the atom was first unlocked. Above the door is an inscription from the Bible: "Great are the works of the Lord. They are pondered by all who delight in them."[8] Modern European science emerged out of a Christian tradition in which the world was understood to be created by God according to laws which were accessible to our reason, and that by uncovering them we were engaged in a noble, God-given task. This was commonly expressed in the idea that God had given humanity two books to learn about him from—the book of Scripture (the Bible), and the book of nature which was "read"

7. Collins, *Language of God*, 1.

8. Ps 111:2.

by scientific endeavor. For example, two of the towering figures of modern astronomy were Galileo and Kepler. Galileo said that "A hundred passages of holy scripture . . . teach us that the glory and greatness of Almighty God are marvellously discerned in all his works and divinely read in the open book of heaven." After Galileo published a book outlining new astronomical discoveries, Kepler wrote an enthusiastic letter to him exclaiming that, after learning of these previously "undisclosed treasures of Jehovah the Creator," which he had revealed through Galileo's work, "Who is not filled with a surging love of God, pouring itself copiously forth through pen and tongue?"[9] As Francis Collins's example shows, many scientists continue to locate themselves in this tradition. In 1916, a study of American scientists found some 40 percent believed in a creator God who answers prayers; when the study was replicated in 1996, almost exactly the same result was returned.[10]

Indeed, twentieth-century science has strengthened the arguments for a creator God. Christians had long reasoned that something can't come from nothing, and that everything must have a beginning, unless, by its nature, it is self-existent, the cause of everything—God himself. Up until the middle of the last century, atheists either challenged this or suggested that the universe, by the same argument, could be eternal. However, the theory of the "Big Bang"—that all matter came into being from a single expanding point and from a single moment around 14 billion years ago—showed that the universe had a beginning and this therefore implied the existence of a creator. Some atheist scientists initially opposed the theory for this reason.

Furthermore, our understanding of the "fine tuning" of the universe after the Big Bang has provided other clues to God's existence. There are many examples of this, but a well-known one is the balance between the energy released in the Big Bang pushing matter outwards, and the force of gravity working in the other direction. If the balance was too powerful in favor of the first, then it is unlikely that galaxies, stars, and planets would have been able

9. Alexander, *Rebuilding the Matrix*, 83–84.

10. Larsen and Witham, "Scientists Are Still Keeping the Faith," 435–36.

to form. If too strong in favor of the latter, then gravity would have pulled all matter back into a single point. Either way, we would not have existed. Owen Gingerich, Professor of Astronomy at Harvard University, said the initial balance had to be accurate to "a ratio of 1 to 1-followed-by-fifty-nine-zeros, an unimaginably large number . . . it seems as if the universe must have been expressly designed for humankind . . . Surely a beneficent Creator was at work to produce a universe fit for intelligent life!"[11] Sir Fred Hoyle, the Cambridge astronomer who coined the phrase "Big Bang" and who was not himself a Christian, said in an article he wrote giving a big-picture overview of our best understanding of the science of the universe that: "A common sense interpretation of the facts suggests that a super-intellect has monkeyed with physics, as well as with chemistry and biology, and that there are no blind forces worth speaking about in nature." He concluded the article emphatically stating his opinion that "The numbers one calculates from the facts seem to me so overwhelming as to put this conclusion almost beyond question."[12] In their recent book on the same subject, the aptly named *A Fortunate Universe,* astrophysicists Geraint Lewis and Luke Barnes put it in a more down-to-earth way when they say that, "we appear to be the result of a cosmic gamble that makes winning EuroMillions look like a dead certainty—a rather unsettling thought!"[13]

Similar arguments can be made from a range of scientific fields as our understanding of the universe has grown. When I was a teenager, I read the arguments of leading atheist thinker Anthony Flew. However, not long after the mapping of the human genome he announced his conversion to a belief in God, based solely on scientific evidence. He concluded that studies of DNA "have shown, by the almost unbelievable complexity of the arrangements which are needed to produce (life), that intelligence must have

---

11. Gingerich, *God's Universe,* 49–50.
12. Hoyle, "Universe," 12.
13. Lewis and Barnes, *Fortunate Universe,* 290.

been involved."[14] The existence and nature of the universe is a clue to God's existence.

Anthropological (Human) Evidence

We have seen that the scientific evidence about the nature of the universe can point us to God's existence. Similarly, the *anthropological* evidence—that is, the common fundamental experience of being human—offers a second set of clues to the existence of God.

In the previous chapter I argued that the universality of the search for meaning is a clue to God's existence, using my own experiences and observations of how different people in different contexts sensed a void of meaning in their lives which they tried to fill in different ways. Anthropologist Ernest Becker wrote in his 1975 book *Escape From Evil* that "Man transcends death by not only continuing to feed his appetites, but especially by finding a meaning for his life, some kind of larger scheme into which he fits."[15] Pope John Paul II put it well in his reflections on the relationship between faith and reason, saying that "in the far reaches of the human heart there is a seed of desire and nostalgia for God."[16]

We see this longing for meaning in every sphere of human activity, including philosophy, literature, music, politics, and our own daily lives. It is particularly clear in religion. Religious belief is one of the most profound and widespread ways in which humans seek to find meaning to their lives and the world, and the ubiquity of religious belief itself is an indication of that "nostalgia for God" that John Paul referred to. Have you ever wondered what we should make of the sheer multitude of religious beliefs in human history? Most societies have had their specific ideas about gods, devils, angels, and divinities. For example, my work at Newcastle University regularly takes me to Denmark, Cyprus, and Central Asia. Each of these places has historically recognized a plethora of

14. Smith, "Atheist Finds 'God' after 50 Years," para. 6.

15. Becker, *Escape from Evil*, 3.

16. John Paul II, *Fides et Ratio*, sec. 24.

religious beliefs. Denmark's old Norse gods like Odin, Thor, and Freya gave us the names of days of the week we still use in the English language—Wednesday, Thursday and Friday. Newcastle and Wallsend are the northernmost outpost of the Roman Empire, whose gods including Mars and Janus gave us the names of the months of the year like March and January. As part of the Greek cultural realm, Cyprus recognized the Greek pantheon of gods, and is itself particularly associated with Aphrodite, the goddess of love. In premodern times Central Asia was occupied by numerous tribal states, each with their own set of gods and religious beliefs that often focused on fertility. Subsequently these became overlaid and replaced with missionary religions such as Buddhism, Christianity, and Islam.[17] Wherever we look, we find religion. As a 2008 article in *The Economist* put it, religion "is a ubiquitous phenomenon—arguably one of the species markers of *Homo sapiens*."[18]

Some sceptics have tried to argue that this is evidence against committed religious belief. Austin Cline makes this point in an article entitled "Too Many Religions, Too Many Gods?" where he writes, "When we look at the great diversity of religions we should notice that they are all incompatible. To put it simply: they can't all be true, but they can all be false." According to Cline, this means that there is no "good, sound, rational, reasonable basis" for identifying one claim about God as true.[19]

But it is perhaps more plausible to draw a different conclusion. If only a single or a few societies in history had ever believed in gods, that would be easier to dismiss as a random anomaly. In contrast, the sheer profusion of beliefs about the divine—arising independently and almost universally in unconnected societies—is one of the most remarkable and extraordinary elements of human history. It demands an explanation. It is hard for atheists to explain religion as simply a product of the evolving, developing brain for, as New Atheists like Christopher Hitchens like to claim, as in the subtitle of one of his books, "Religion poisons everything"

17. Foltz, *Religions of the Silk Road.*
18. "Science of Religion," 103–5.
19. Cline, "Too Many Gods?," para. 11.

and retards human development.[20] A more reasonable explanation is that we are made by God with an inbuilt knowledge of and desire for him that bubbles out in a multitude of different beliefs and practices. In one of his poems, Francis Quarles (1592–1644) likens the human soul to the magnetic needle of a compass that seems to swing from one side to another, until:

> Thus finding all the world's delight to be
> But empty toys, good God! She points alone to thee.[21]

As we saw in the last chapter, the Bible claims that God "has put eternity in their [human] hearts,"[22] that is, that he made us with a fundamental orientation towards himself. The anthropological evidence of both the universal search for meaning and the existence of a great diversity of religions is a clue to God's existence. The Christian gospel "makes sense of the enigmas of our experience," suggests Oxford University professor Alister McGrath, a former atheist who came to faith in Jesus.[23]

Cambridge University geneticist Denis Alexander makes the pointed claim that:

> atheism fails to convince: as a metaphysical system it involves a profound mismatch between commitment to a life in which goals and achievements are deemed to carry some significance, and a worldview in which the existence of life itself must, by definition, be ultimately futile.[24]

Pondering this anthropological evidence has led many people (including me) to conclude that the existence of God makes better sense of all the human (anthropological) evidence than his absence. The search for God and for meaning and purpose in our lives is commonplace across human history, and is a clue to the existence of God.

---

20. Hitchens, *God Is Not Great*.
21. Quarles, *Quarles' Emblems*, 202.
22. Eccl 3:11.
23. McGrath, *Surprised by Meaning*, 100.
24. Alexander, *Rebuilding the Matrix*, 247–48.

Morality

A third clue to God's existence is morality. During a 2020 CO-VID-19 lockdown my family spent a lot more time in our garden. At least, we regarded it as our garden, but a certain male pigeon, whom we nicknamed "Terry," had other ideas. He considered it to be his territory and used his strength and size to chase away all other male pigeons. This enabled him to gobble up more than his fair share of the bread we put out each day on the bird table, maintain his strength with minimum effort, and then use these advantages to mate with a female pigeon. We were not happy with what we saw as this selfish behavior, as other birds went without. But Terry himself was more generous in his attitude towards us, graciously allowing us to continue to share his garden!

We were unreasonable and sentimental to censure Terry's behavior as morally objectionable—it is survival of the fittest, the result of his inborn, natural impulses. However, we expect very different standards of behavior from people. For example, in February 2020, as the spread of the COVID-19 virus was accelerating into a pandemic, Hollywood film producer Harvey Weinstein was sentenced to twenty-three years in prison for sexual abuse of women in the film industry. This was welcomed by people who had campaigned on this issue for years, angry that his strength (based on his wealth and power) had enabled him to evade justice for so long. An array of campaigners took to the airwaves to express their relief and pleasure at the verdict. This was not vindictive—it was a satisfaction that he had been brought to justice. This is because we instinctively know that there is a moral law in the universe, and that, unlike animals, no one should be able to evade it by their wealth and privilege. This is the third clue, the third piece of evidence, pointing us towards the existence of God.

The *Monty Python* sketch with which we began this chapter was a satire, I suspect, of a famous 1948 BBC radio debate between Bishop Fred Copleston and atheist philosopher Bertrand Russell. When the debate moved on to discuss morality, Russell said he thought there was good and bad in the universe but that he didn't need a concept of "Divine goodness" to help explain that. Copleston asked Russell, "What's your justification for distinguishing between good and bad?" Russell replied:

> I don't have any justification any more than I have when I distinguish between blue and yellow. What is my justification for distinguishing between blue and yellow? I can see they are different.[25]

Copleston pounced on this: "Well, that is an excellent justification, I agree," he said. "You distinguish blue and yellow by seeing them, so you distinguish good and bad by what faculty?" Russell could only answer, "By my feelings."

This is a flimsy and unconvincing response. Russell was a cultured and privileged member of the English aristocracy who had been brought up on decent, solid English morality that had been moulded for centuries by Christian culture. He was, due to the society he was cultivated in and the privilege that he had access to, unlikely to do anything desperately outrageous. But as Harvey Weinstein said in his defense, he felt that he was acting properly. Stalin and Hitler and every other tyrant has no doubt felt the same, that their actions were justifiable. How can we judge? If there is no God to set the standards of good and evil, then the distinction between right and wrong is just down to our feelings—or, worse, it is down to who has the strength to enforce their feelings of right on others.

In his book *Mere Christianity*, C. S. Lewis wrote of this inbuilt sense of morality, or "moral law":

> If there was a controlling power outside the universe, it could not show itself to us as one of the facts inside the universe—no more than the architect of a house could actually be a wall or staircase or fireplace in that house. The only way in which we could expect it to show itself would be inside us as an influence or a command trying to get us to behave in a certain way. And that is just what

25. Russell and Copleston, "Transcript," para. 98.

we do find inside ourselves. Surely this ought to arouse
our suspicions?[26]

Francis Collins—whom as we saw earlier led the Human Genome Project—had previously been an atheist, but recalled how, as
a young scientist, he was stunned when he read this passage from
Lewis. The daily experience of the moral law, he recalled, "shone its
bright white light into the recesses of my childish atheism"—and
this was a key moment in persuading him that belief in God was
more reasonable and made better sense of the scientific and moral
evidence than unbelief.[27]

God Has Communicated to Us in Jesus Christ

So far we have considered three clues to the existence of God:
science, anthropology, and morality. These are general clues that
could be true of an understanding of God as shared by Christianity, Judaism, Islam, and some other religions. We will finish by
looking at one more clue that points specifically to the Christian
understanding of God—that God has communicated himself to
humanity in Jesus Christ as portrayed in the Bible.

In 1995, American singer-songwriter Joan Osborne's debut
album contained what became an unlikely hit song, the haunting
"What if God Was One of Us?" The chorus acknowledged that
God is "good" and "great," but insisted on asking how different it
would look if God was one of us. The point she makes is an excellent one. However convincing we may find the arguments about
the scientific and anthropological evidence ("God is great") and
the origins of morality ("God is good"), that still makes God seem
distant and remote. But the Bible's claim is precisely that in Jesus
Christ God *did* become one of us.

An obvious question is: how do we know this, how can we
trust the Bible? Can't we dismiss Jesus as a myth? That Jesus was
a real person there can be little doubt, as he is mentioned in the

26. Lewis, *Mere Christianity*, 32.
27. Collins, *Language of God*, 29.

historical writings of his non-Christian Jesus contemporary, the historian Josephus. But listen to the claim made by Luke, the writer of one of the Gospels (the first-hand accounts of Jesus Christ's life):

> Many have undertaken to draw up an account of the things that have been fulfilled among us, just as they were handed down to us by those who from the first were eyewitnesses and servants of the word. Therefore, since I myself have carefully investigated everything from the beginning, it seemed good also to me to write an orderly account for you, most excellent Theophilus, so that you may know the certainty of the things you have been taught.[28]

This doesn't sound like the genre of myth, in the way that stories about the Norse and Greek gods are written. The New Testament claims to present reliable history. Biblical scholar F.F. Bruce suggests that "There is no body of ancient literature in the world which enjoys such a wealth of good textual attestation as the New Testament."[29] For example, each year I begin a set of undergraduate lectures on the history of geographical thought by discussing the work of Greek philosopher Plato. No one has ever challenged me as to whether Plato existed or whether the texts we have of his work are accurate enough to enable me to discuss them meaningfully. Yet Yale University Library's Plato Microfilm Project lists just over 200 known Plato manuscripts, the earliest dating to around 1200 years after he lived.[30] In contrast, scholars at the Institute for New Testament Textual Research in Münster have tallied nearly 5,800 New Testament manuscripts, the earliest of which is believed to date to only 100 years after the life of Christ.[31] This does not prove that the Bible's claims are true, but as James Prothro argues it shows that "what we have for the New Testament is not simply *more* reliable than what we have for Plato but that what we have is simply *reliable.*"[32]

---

28. Luke 1:1–4.
29. Bruce, *Books and the Parchments*, 178.
30. Clay, "The bibliographical test updated," para. 12.
31. Clay, "The bibliographical test updated," para. 20.
32. Prothro. "Myths About Classical Literature," 88 (italics original).

The New Testament claims that in Jesus Christ, to use the words of Joan Osborne's song, God indeed did become "one of us." He lived, taught about who God was, performed miracles that were evidence of his divinity, and provided answers to the big questions about meaning, purpose, suffering, and death. He died on the cross and rose again in the greatest miracle of all—a miracle that was seen by numerous eyewitnesses. The New Testament explains that Jesus died and rose again to take the punishment our sins deserved and thus allow us to enter into a real relationship with God, the Creator of the universe. We will consider this in more detail in the next two chapters, but the point is that God has not merely left clues to his existence in science, anthropology, and morality, but rather has personally stepped into our world to communicate directly to us.

Narnia and God in the Lockdown

Like many people, I saw more films during the COVID-19 pandemic than I usually would. My family and I started the first lockdown by watching a number of movies based on C. S. Lewis's Narnia chronicles. Lewis, a scholar of English Literature at Oxford and Cambridge Universities, wrote the stories as an allegory of the Christian faith. Lewis himself was an atheist who became a Christian after being persuaded by some of the anthropological evidence for the existence of God. In his autobiography, *Surprised by Joy,* he described himself as "the most dejected and reluctant convert in all England."[33] What he meant was that he didn't want to be a Christian, but he was honest enough to follow where the evidence took him. In this chapter we've looked briefly at some of that evidence: scientific, anthropological, moral, and the coming into the world of Jesus Christ as set out in the Bible. This evidence, and more, led me to conclude that, in response to this important question about whether we can know God exists, belief in God is

---

33. Lewis, *Surprised by Joy,* 182.

more reasonable and rational than unbelief because it makes better sense of the evidence.

Actually, C. S. Lewis probably wouldn't have approved of my description of this question as simply "important." He famously said: "Christianity is a statement which, if false, is of *no* importance, and, if true, of infinite importance. The one thing it cannot be is moderately important."[34] This is because of the consequences. If the God of the Bible exists, this has profound implications for the understanding of our meaning and purpose on earth, how we value and live life, the ways we approach suffering and death, and even our eternal destinies. Nothing could be more important than answering this question, yet it is one that we too often push to the back of our minds as we fill our lives with busyness. A crisis like World War Two, the 2007-8 financial collapse, the 2022 Russian invasion of Ukraine, or the Coronavirus pandemic, which so unsettle our everyday realities, makes it harder than usual to avoid asking it.

You may be wondering about the outcome of the *Monty Python* wrestling-match debate about God's existence with which we began this chapter. At the end of the episode in which the sketch occurred, the usual final credits rolled, and then a voiceover announced: "And here is the result of *The Epilogue*—God exists by two falls to a submission!"[35] I think that there are better reasons for being able to conclude that God exists.

---

34. Lewis, "Christian Apologetics," 101 (italics original).
35. Chapman et al, *Monty Python's Flying Circus*, 28.

3

If There's a God, Why Does He
Allow Terrible Crises to Happen?

As COVID-19 LOCKDOWNS CAME into force across the world in early 2020, the numbers of people subscribing to film and TV home streaming services soared. The Disney+ channel saw an almost doubling of its viewers from 26.5 million in December 2019 to over 50 million by the following April, as people stuck at home binged on its mixture of Star Wars and Marvel superhero back catalogs.[1] Superhero movies are a staple of the silver screen nowadays, but when I was a child the genre barely existed. I remember watching the first-ever Superman movie, made in 1978 and starring Christopher Reeves. The plot revolves around a plan by criminal genius Lex Luthor to target two nuclear missiles on cities in the USA. Superman manages to stop one of them, but not the second, which hits California, killing many people including his love interest Lois Lane. Angered at not being able to prevent this, Superman speeds round the earth going back in time and saving both California and Lois. In doing so, Superman proves that he is powerful, and that he is good.

1. Bursztynsky, "Disney Says," para. 1.

I think that's often the twin-standard by which we judge God, and is the assumption behind the question of this chapter: "If there's a God, why does he allow bad things to happen?" The argument, restated in various ways by different people over time, runs like this. If God is too weak to stop bad things happening, he's not much of a god. On the other hand, if he could stop them but chooses not to, then he's not morally good. Either way, he is not a being we could or should respect or worship. British actor Stephen Fry was thinking along these lines when he responded to a question on Irish television in 2015 put by chat show host Gay Byrne about what he would say if he met God. He answered simply, "Bone cancer in children?" Then he went on to elaborate:

> "What's that about? How dare you! How dare you create a world in which there is such suffering that is not our fault? It's not right, it's utterly, utterly evil. Why should I respect a capricious, mean-minded, stupid god, who creates a world which is so full of injustice and pain?" That's what I would say.[2]

I do not know whether Fry was thinking of a particular child when he said that, but the emotion and anger in his response is a reminder that this question of why God would allow suffering is never just an intellectual one. It's deeply personal. We all know what it's like to feel overwhelmed by suffering. The terrible loneliness of being without people who understand us. The ache of disappointment at missing out on the dream job. The immobilizing fear of seeing a bully's evil smile as he or she walks towards us across the playground or office. The unbearable yearning of being in love with someone who doesn't return that feeling. The inconsolable grief of having a loved one suddenly taken by some terrible tragedy, or watching them slowly die of an incurable disease. As humans, we know these all too well.

Many of us feel the sharpness of such suffering more clearly during a crisis like the COVID-19 pandemic. By the autumn of 2021, as I revised this paragraph, Brown University's Costs of War

2. Perry, "Stephen Fry Says," para. 3.

project estimated that nearly 1 million people had died in "the post-9/11 wars due to direct war violence, and several times as many due to the reverberating effects of war."[3] On top of that, these wars had produced around 38 million refugees and displaced persons. At the same time, the COVID-19 pandemic had taken around 4 million lives globally, as well as subjecting societies and individuals to fear, disruption, loneliness, sickness, unemployment, and financial hardship. Where is God in all this? Why doesn't he come in like Superman and make it all right? If he is almighty, why has he made a world in which such suffering occurs?

I am not going to offer easy answers to this question, as I do not think that such answers exist. But I want to start by thinking about the way we ask the question itself, and then move on to four reflections that Christians draw from the Bible to help us address the question.

The Question Itself Points to God

Historian Mike Davies wrote a book called *Late Victorian Holocausts* about mass deaths by famine and drought in India under British imperial rule. It is a powerful text, combining climatic data and careful archival research with searing moral clarity to argue that people died not because of tragic natural disasters but rather political choices. The British Empire ran India for its own economic benefit rather than the welfare of the population, and it was actually exporting grain from India to the UK as tens of millions of Indians starved to death.[4]

Reading the book makes you feel very angry. But what is also interesting is that Davies dedicates it to a late colleague, whose death he regards as "simply an obscenity."[5] That is a very telling choice of words. What basis does he have to be outraged (rather than just grieved) at the suffering of Indians and the death of a friend?

3. Watson Institute, Brown University, "Costs of War."
4. Davies, *Late Victorian Holocausts*.
5. Davies, *Late Victorian Holocausts*, x.

Atheism is unable to help us here. Richard Dawkins, outspoken pop atheist and retired Oxford University biology professor, said this:

> In a universe of blind physical forces and genetic replication, some people are going to get hurt, other people are going to get lucky, and you won't find any rhyme or reason in it, nor any justice. The universe we observe has precisely the properties we should expect if there is, at bottom, no design, no purpose, no evil and no good, nothing but blind pitiless indifference.[6]

Why do we get angry at suffering and regard it as so outrageous? Dawkins's pointed words show that such anger makes no sense for atheism because that is just how the world is. As we saw in chapter 1, if we don't believe that humans were made "in the image of God" we cannot claim that they have any intrinsic value. When faced with personal or global crises, atheism's arguments about suffering ring too hollow for us to accept. With Mike Davies, we still ask the question about why suffering occurs. But who is it that are we asking? Could it be that we ask "why?" because, deep down, we know that God is real?

Could God Have Made a World without Suffering?

I once saw a sweatshirt sporting a classic quip attributed to humorist Jack Handey: "I can picture in my mind a world without war, a world without hate. And I can picture us attacking that world because they'd never expect it." The question about why God allows suffering is one that asks us to picture in our minds a world without war, hatred, coronaviruses, bullying, imperialism, drought, cancer, traffic accidents, or any other form of suffering, and then ask, if God is so powerful and good, why he didn't make that world? But on closer examination this is not as simple as it sounds. What would that world look like?

6. Dawkins, *River Out of Eden*, 133.

In the Bible's view, we are responsible to God for our actions. It's part of what makes us humans. The first instance of moral evil (that is, humans doing bad things to other humans) in the Bible is the murder of Abel by Cain, in Genesis 4. Both men, the sons of Adam and Eve, offer sacrifices to God and, for reasons that aren't quite clear to the reader, God accepted Abel's sacrifice but not Cain's. Cain broods with murderous fury, and God says to him:

> Why are you angry? Why is your face downcast? If you do what is right, will you not be accepted? But if you do not do what is right, sin is crouching at your door; it desires to have you, but you must rule over it.[7]

Cain ignored God's warning and killed his brother. God could have stopped him, but he gave him a choice and invited him to use it well. He still gives us choices and delegates to us the responsibility of looking after so many aspects of his world. By doing that he risks us making bad choices and misusing that responsibility. In demanding a world without suffering, are we saying that we don't want that responsibility? Do we want a God who, when we are chatting to a friend and start bad-mouthing someone, suddenly switches us on to mute? Who, if we are on the verge of dropping litter, makes the empty drinks can stick in our hands? When, if we are about to think an angry or lustful thought about a colleague at a meeting, stops the thought from forming? Instead, do we want a God who would make us write and say and think and do only good things? That would stop a lot of suffering—but at what cost? Sharon Dirckx pointedly puts the problem of conjuring such a world:

> Perhaps much evil would be prevented, but the inability to make any form of meaningful decision might itself lead to meaninglessness and despair, and contempt for the God who treats people like puppets or pieces on a chessboard.[8]

Dirckx suggests that the thought-provoking 1998 film *The Truman Show* can help us clarify this. Truman Burbank is the

7. Gen 4:6–7.
8. Dirckx, *Why?*, 57.

unsuspecting star of a reality TV drama. Adopted by the production company at birth as an orphan, he thinks he is living a real life with a job as an insurance salesman, a nice home and car, a beautiful wife, and great friends. But it is all a vast TV show that has been running for three decades. Everyone around him is an actor, and thousands of secret cameras are filming his every action for a worldwide audience.

The film follows him as realization at what is truly happening dawns, and after several failed attempts he makes a successful break for freedom. He is challenged by the show's demonic producer, Kristoff, who says, "In my world you have nothing to fear"[9]—a completely safe world, why would he want to leave it? But Truman ignores Kristoff, and the film finishes with the powerful symbolism of Truman walking off set and out of the door into the real world. As Truman pauses to decide what to do, the viewer is urging him on to do that. A world in which people can only choose to do good because God has programmed them that way isn't a world that is morally free and responsible. Would that be a cost worth paying for a world without suffering?

So perhaps God had good reasons for allowing the suffering of moral evil. But isn't what we call natural evil (human suffering not caused by human action) different? Why didn't God make a world without viruses like smallpox, flu, ebola, and coronavirus?

What at first seems a simple point becomes more complicated when we look at what viruses are and do. In April 2020, Hugh Harris, a microbiologist at University College Cork, wrote an article entitled "In Defence of Viruses." He explains how the more we understand them, the more scientists are "starting to view them as an essential component of microbial ecosystems."[10] There are 100 million viral types on earth, and only a few are harmful to humans. Many more are useful. Viruses prevent bacteria taking over the environment, they recycle nutrients, they live in our guts to maintain our immune system, and in an age where more and more diseases are becoming immune to antibiotics, fighting

9. Weir, *Truman Show*, 1:33:06–1:33:11.

10. Harris, "In Defence of Viruses," para. 8.

bacteria with viruses is being explored as a promising strategy to help prevent future pandemics and also to develop new treatments for immunodeficiency viruses like HIV. Professor Peter Pollard of Griffith University says "viruses make the world go round"—they are "our smallest unsung heroes."[11] Again, do we want a God who constantly and repeatedly performs millions of little supernatural miracles to stop virus actions or transmissions that are harmful to humans? That might actually hinder our understanding of viruses and harm our medical research. Science depends on experiments being replicable, that is, they can be repeated and the same outcome happens each time. If God kept changing the outcomes and we didn't know when, research on finding cures or vaccines for viruses might be hindered. Maybe God had good reasons for making the world as it is. Simply because we don't yet understand them, doesn't mean they don't exist.

I have argued that this heartfelt and often painful question of why is there so much suffering only makes sense if there is a God, and the question as to why he didn't make a world without suffering turns out to be more complicated that it sounds. But what might Christians say more positively about suffering? The Bible never explicitly poses the question "Why does God allow suffering?" in the way we do, and in the remainder of this chapter I want to consider four reflections that Christians have often used to approach the question: that we are not meant to suffer, that God is with us in our suffering, that he uses suffering for good, and that eventually suffering will be expunged from the universe.

We Are Not Meant to Suffer

The Bible opens with a suffering-free universe. Its creation narrative in the early chapters of the book of Genesis portrays a world that was, as the first chapter of the Bible repeatedly says, "good." The first humans lived together in the paradise of Eden without

---

11. Pollard, "Viruses Don't Deserve Their Bad Rap," para. 20.

mistrust (they were naked and yet "felt no shame"[12]), pain, or death, in close relationship with God and with the animals who were unafraid of them. When God looked at the world, "he saw that it was very good."[13]

To grasp what this says about suffering it is helpful to contrast it with other contemporary ancient Near East creation stories. In the *Enuma Elish* Babylonian myth, the universe is created from the bloody corpse of the slain god Tiamat following a fierce battle between competing deities. In this account, evil and suffering and death are primordial to the universe, along with good. Humans were created from the divine blood, in order to serve the gods. Scholars have argued that these myths legitimized hierarchical, unequal, and violent societies.[14] In Genesis, pain and suffering, hierarchical human relations, and death itself, are entirely absent at creation. They were not part of God's good design for us.

Instead, Genesis locates all kinds of suffering in our world as a result of human disobedience. The first human beings, Adam and Eve, are portrayed as breaking God's command not to eat from "the tree of the knowledge of good and evil" otherwise they would suffer death.[15] The consequences of this, as God had warned them, were dire. Expulsion from paradise, separation from the presence of God, shame and embarrassment with each other, physical pain, frustration in work, alienation from animals, warped gender relations, interhuman violence and, ultimately, death, all ensued (Gen 3–4). In the New Testament, Paul claims in his letter to the church in Rome that "creation itself" was subject to "bondage and decay" because of this sin.[16] Our relationship with the very environment in which we live has been distorted, so that instead of sustaining us the natural world is often a source of suffering for us—for example, through viruses or extreme weather conditions.

12. Gen 2:25.
13. Gen 1:31.
14. Middleton, *Liberating Image*, ch. 4.
15. Gen 2:17.
16. Rom 8:20–21.

It should be acknowledged that different theologians interpret the early chapters of Genesis differently.[17] But however we understand such passages, they point to a key idea that death, pain, and suffering of all kinds are not meant to be intrinsic to life, and they invite us to imagine a world marked by their absence. Mike Davis was right: death is "simply an obscenity." We *should* feel angry about and grieved at suffering. Instead of atheism's monumental shrug in the face of the universe's "blind pitiless indifference" to our suffering, Christianity insists that suffering and pain are *not* just inevitable facts of life—they are evidence of creation askew. The rest of the Bible's story is the story of what God is doing about them.

God Is with Us in Suffering

One of the greatest comforts to us when we suffer is to be supported by people who understand what we are going through. They may be friends and family, strangers on telephone help lines, or people in a support group suffering the same kind of illness or trauma that we or our families are facing. I experienced this most vividly in my life during the period I described in chapter 1, when I was searching for meaning in life. The pain I was feeling was intensified by conversations with different friends who simply could not understand, and reacted angrily to me: "Stop reading those books!" one said, as though all my questions would disappear if I just ceased thinking. I stopped talking to people about what was happening, feeling not only deeply hurt but also misunderstood and lonely. In contrast a friend, Chris, was an inestimable help to me because he was able to listen with understanding and care, having experienced something similar himself. I went to spend three days with him, during which he listened carefully to me for hours and hours. He didn't resolve things, and neither were there blinding lights from heaven, but because he had "been there and done that" and had come through it, he was able to sympathize with and encourage me, leaving me feeling more hopeful and less alone.

17. Alexander, *Creation or Evolution?*, ch. 11.

When we are experiencing suffering, we often find most comfort by talking to people who have gone through the same thing.

The Bible presents Jesus to us in that way. His thirty-three years on earth were marked by suffering. He began life as a refugee, his parents fleeing to Egypt to escape the genocidal tyranny of King Herod. After returning home to Palestine, he grew up experiencing national humiliation under an oppressive occupying power—the Romans, whose violent reign stretched all the way from North Africa and Palestine up to their wall here at Newcastle and Wallsend, where I live. He had no partner, and was regarded by many including his family as mentally unstable. He felt sorrow and grief, the Bible's shortest verse recording simply that "Jesus wept" at the death of his friend Lazarus.[18] Ultimately he was wrongly accused, betrayed, and abandoned by his friends, and suffered an excruciating death. The Bible describes him as "a man of suffering, and familiar with pain."[19]

Think how different this view of God is from the most common human ideas about the divinity. The ancient Greeks saw God as an 'unmoved mover.' By 'mover' they meant he was all-powerful, the creator and originator of everything who set the world and human history moving. By 'unmoved' they meant he was distant and so far exalted above us that he was not moved or troubled by our sufferings. Most religions have seen God in that way—he is too glorious or remote to be emotionally bothered about us. The Bible's understanding is startlingly different. The Bible says that in Jesus God "understands our weaknesses, for he faced all of the same testings we do."[20] He knows what our pain-filled lives are like. He gets it. He is thus uniquely equipped to journey through difficulties and pain with us. People down the ages have found this fact to be a great comfort to help them live through suffering.

18. John 11:35.

19. Isa 53:3.

20. Heb 4:15 NLT.

God Uses Suffering for Good

A third biblical insight on suffering is that although God is not its author, as sovereign ruler of the universe he can use suffering for good. When the COVID-19 lockdown began, Andrew Lloyd Webber began streaming his popular musicals online in a series for Broadway and West End fans in the UK to enjoy free of charge. Entitled, "The Shows Must Go On," the series began with his famous *Joseph and the Amazing Technicolor Dreamcoat*.[21] A star-studded cast retold a version of the biblical story of Joseph. Jacob has twelve sons, but, in a classic example of how not to parent, he treats the youngest, Joseph, as his clear favourite. This is symbolized by making him a wonderful "richly ornamented robe."[22] Understandably jealous, his brothers rough him up and sell him into slavery, telling his distraught father that he was killed by wild animals. Joseph is taken to Egypt, and works his way up to become head of the government, saving Egypt from a famine. As the famine bites across the region, his brothers travel to Egypt for humanitarian aid, and although they come before Joseph to plead for grain they do not recognize him. At the dramatic climax of the story, Joseph reveals his identity to them, saying, "You intended to harm me, but God intended it for good to accomplish what is now being done, the saving of many lives."[23]

This is an idea that is often found in the Bible, and which Christians down the ages have also experienced—that God uses suffering and pain and evil human intentions to bring about good. God is never the author of evil, but rather he permits evil to work and overrules it for his wise and holy purposes. Ultimately, God is sovereign and is able to make everything, including the result of all the evil of all time, work together for a greater good: "in all things God works for the good of those who love him," Paul claims boldly in his Letter to the Romans.[24]

21. Wood, "Andrew Lloyd Webber."
22. Gen 37:3.
23. Gen 50:20.
24. Rom 8:28.

At times some people have interpreted natural or political disasters as specific punishments of God. This is not new. In Luke 13, Jesus comments on some worshipers from the Galilee region who had been massacred by Pontius Pilate, and on eighteen people who died when the Tower of Siloam collapsed on them. In both cases Jesus asked if their deaths were because they were particularly bad sinners: "No, I tell you" was his answer.[25] As John Lennox observes, Jesus is discussing both moral evil (an atrocity perpetrated by a murderous tyrant) and natural evil (the outworking of geophysical laws).[26] In the same way, we cannot say that God engineered the COVID-19 pandemic, the "War on Terror," the global financial crash, or other crises—but he is able to bring good from them. Initial COVID-19 lockdown measures around the world saw things like the homeless in England housed overnight,[27] and trafficked sex-workers liberated as "red-light districts" in India closed down.[28] Why can't we do that long term? As Archbishop of Canterbury, Justin Welby, observed in his Easter 2021 sermon, following the pandemic life can either "go on as before," with a society that fails so many, "Or we can go with the flooding life and purpose of the resurrection of Jesus, which changes all things, and choose a better future for all."[29]

Redemption and Restoration

The promise that God is with us in hardship and will use it for good helps us practically in a way that atheism's view of suffering as blind indifference never could. But, nonetheless, I don't think that this answers all our questions. We still want to ask: Why doesn't God just get rid of evil once and for all? The Bible's answer is—that's exactly what he is doing! He did it on the cross, and when

---

25. Luke 13:1–4.

26. Lennox, *Where Is God in a Coronavirus World?*, 24.

27. Cromarty, *Coronavirus.*

28. Ashcraft, "Pandemic Shuts Down Red Light Districts in India."

29. Waterson, "Choose a Better Future for All," para. 3.

Jesus Christ returns to earth at the end of time the effects of that work will be finally completed.

The cross is central to biblical faith. In the Bible's narrative, the power of evil was defeated on that first Easter, and one day it will be removed altogether at the end of time when Jesus comes back. On the cross, Jesus bore our sorrows and weaknesses and all the wrong choices we have made as individuals and a race, and all the consequences of those for ourselves, our society, and our environment. He took the punishment that we deserve for our wrongdoing. By believing in him we can experience forgiveness and have a personal relationship with God.

But this redemption is also the grounds for the future ending of all suffering—restoration. The final book of the Bible, Revelation, puts it like this: "He will wipe every tear from their eyes. There will be no more death, or mourning or crying or pain, for the old order of things has passed away."[30] This is a beautiful image of a tender God and his plan to deal with all that's wrong with the world—including deadly viruses, wars, genocides, terror attacks, and natural or industrial calamities.

That can be hard for us to imagine, as we often think of a future afterlife as some sort of slightly unreal dream of angels with harps floating around on cotton-wool clouds. The biblical idea is much closer to James Cameron's Oscar-winning 2009 science-fiction film *Avatar*. Set in the twenty-second century, it tells the story of Jake Sully, a wheelchair-bound former soldier who cannot afford the spinal operation that would restore the use of his paralyzed legs. He signs up for a project where the militarized Resources Development Administration (RDA) is extracting "unobtanium" from the thickly-forested planet of Pandora, to make up for earth's energy crisis. The only thing that stands in the way is the Na'vi, a race of tall, humanoid, blue-skinned inhabitants whose ancestral lands contain the richest seams of unobtanium. To get round this the corporation has created avatars looking just like the natives, but genetically-modified to partially resemble Jake Sully and the other people who operate them remotely from special

---

30. Rev 21:4.

capsules in their heavily fortified base. This genetic modification allows the operators to merge their minds with the avatar bodies. The purpose of the Avatar Program is to ingratiate the RDA with the Na'vi and persuade them to leave their sacred lands and move elsewhere, to allow the mining to go ahead.

There is an unforgettable and breathtaking scene when Sully first operates his avatar. He is lifted from his wheelchair into the operating capsule, and nodes are placed on his head to control the avatar from his brain. When the procedure begins, he falls unconscious but wakes up as the avatar, fully inhabiting its now activated body. After some faltering steps, he moves outside into the training ground and runs wildly and joyfully around, leaping and bounding with his new, powerful legs, thrilling at the sensation of running in a planet teeming with an abundance of natural life. As the film unfolds, Sully explores the extraordinarily lush planet and, with the help of the Na'vi whose trust he wins, discovers that it is a world more vivid and more authentic and more moral than his own. He eventually sides with the Na'vi and helps them defeat the RDA, and the Na'vi attempt a ceremony to transfer his whole life into the avatar. The final shot in the film is when the avatar's eyes flick open as the procedure has worked. Sully is now fully reborn into this new reality, the old still recognizable but made new and better and more alive than ever before.

Revelation is suggesting something similar. Not only will suffering and sickness end, but our future life in the new heavens and the new earth will be more vivid, more alive, more relational, and more real—more everything that is good. So forget the fanciful cartoons of angels with harps on unreal clouds. A far better image is that of Jake Sully's avatar reveling in the rich life of a world he had previously only really glimpsed from a sealed command base, but never fully experienced. On the cross God did address the problem of evil and suffering once and for all, and when Jesus Christ returns to earth at the end of time that work will be finally completed.

Sad Things Coming Untrue

J. R. R. Tolkien wrote a series of books set in the fantasy world of Middle Earth—*The Hobbit* and *The Lord of the Rings*. These describe the ultimately successful efforts of some unlikely heroes, a race of stocky creatures called hobbits, to defeat the evil dark lord, Sauron, who threatens to overwhelm the alliance of free men, elves and dwarves standing against him. At the end of the final book in the series, *The Return of the King*, hobbit Sam Gamgee discovers that his friend Gandalf the wizard was not dead (as he thought) but alive. Sam cries, "I thought you were dead! But then I thought I was dead myself!" And then he exclaims the question "Is everything sad going to come untrue?"[31]

Tolkien—who was himself a Christian—phrases Sam's question superbly, in a way that gets to the heart of this difficult topic about why a good God would allow suffering. As humans, we experience pain and death not as simply part of the natural cycle, but rather as something sad, as objectionable, as a *wrongness in the universe*. Sociologist John Holloway, in his book *Change the World Without Taking Power*, conjures an image of the "global scream" of the oppressed and exploited. In a deeply impressive passage that resonates with the Bible's story, he writes:

> Our anger is directed not just against particular happenings but against a more general wrongness, a feeling that the world is askew, that the world is in some way untrue. When we experience something particularly horrific, we hold up our hands in horror and say 'that cannot be! It cannot be true!' We know that it is true, but feel that it is the truth of an untrue world.[32]

For the consistent atheist, this anger at injustice is mere sentiment and irrationality, for we are just physical material made in the Big Bang and formed into biological organisms by evolution's chance processes of competition, suffering, and death. There is no intrinsic value and nothing to lament about suffering, and because

31. Tolkien, *Return of the King*, 930.
32. Holloway, *Change the World*, 2.

one day the universe's energy will run out and everything will die and there will be no being left to lament it anyway. But we know instinctively that this isn't right. That we ask this very question about suffering is itself one of the clues to God's existence that we saw in the previous chapter. Christians cannot give neat and definitive answers about why God chose to make this universe and give us responsibility and choice, when he knew that we would mess it up and cause so much suffering. We don't know why he allowed the COVID-19 pandemic. But we do know that pain, disease, and death were not part of his good intentions for his people. We know that he is with us in our sufferings because he experienced them himself. We know that God takes our suffering so seriously that he took it upon himself on the cross. We know that he is sovereign and can bring good out of evil. And we know that one day, at the end of time, Jesus Christ will return and remake heaven and earth and bring all suffering to an end.

John Holloway wrote, "We know that it [pain] is true, but feel that it is the truth of an untrue world." This brings us back to Sam Gamgee's question, "Is everything sad going to come untrue?" New York church leader Tim Keller writes this: "The answer of Christianity to that question is—yes. Everything sad is going to come untrue and it will somehow be greater for having once been broken and lost."[33] And as we shall see in the next chapter, this is true of the ultimate suffering we face—death.

33. Keller, *Reason for God,* 32.

4

How Can We Make Sense of Death?

IN AUTUMN 2019, THE anonymous British street-artist Banksy made headlines with a pop-up London store called Gross Domestic Product. Shoppers could acquire items such as a disco glitter ball made into a riot-police helmet, and a ladies' handbag created by handles and a buckle attached to a brick. To my mind the most striking item was a gravestone with the inscription, based on the language of a satnav, "You have now reached your destination."[1] As Banksy intended the store made headlines because it was arresting. Death is always arresting. We know that we will die—our chances of dying are precisely 100 percent—but it simply isn't something that we like to think about.

However, at times of crisis or catastrophe it becomes much harder than usual not to think about death. It is close at hand. Some years ago, I was privileged to stay at the home of and interview Kefa Sempangi, a Ugandan pastor, professor, and politician who fell foul of dictator Idi Amin when he unleashed a catastrophic reign of terror on the country in the 1970s. Sempangi described to me how, at the height of that tyranny, death was everywhere, on every street. On Easter Sunday 1973, at the end of a week in

1. Bakare, "Banksy Launches Homewares Shop."

which he had witnessed terrible instances of cold-blooded murder by Amin's thugs, he found himself alone and confronted by five of these assassins. "We are going to kill you. If you have anything to say, say it before you die," said the leader, his face twisted with hatred. We'll find out what happened next in chapter 5, but under such circumstances no Ugandan could avoid thinking about death. It is the same in any major crisis. On more than one occasion I have spoken on the phone to friends in warzones as the sound of explosions or gunfire rattled in the background: death was close. In an age of terrorism, ghastly reports of mass atrocities in cities we know like New York, Manchester, Paris, Istanbul, and Mumbai remind us that death could just as suddenly strike us when we are out in the streets. In a pandemic like COVID-19, every stranger could potentially deal death to us, and we in turn could pass on a lethal virus to others without even knowing that we carried it.

In crises or catastrophes like these, death is personal, real, and frightening. How do we live with the knowledge that we could die very soon? In this chapter we will look at the Bible's take on death: that it is not meant to be part of the human story, that we can face it well, and that there is life and judgment beyond the grave. These, I argue, can help us live well as we face personal and global crises and catastrophes. We will also ask whether this isn't just wishful thinking and if there is any evidence that the Bible's hope for life after death is true. But first I want to examine how most people respond to death—which is, by trying to ignore or avoid it.

Avoiding Death?

In 2015, relationship therapist Esther Perel gave a much-watched TED talk entitled "Rethinking Infidelity," exploring why people cheat on their partners and how couples maintain healthy, long-term relationships. At one point she made a striking observation: "Some affairs are an attempt to beat back deadness and an antidote to death."[2]

2. Perel, "Rethinking Infidelity," 13:20–13:23.

Perel was far from the first person to note that a lot of what we do in life is avoiding death. It is the central them in Russian author Leo Tolstoy's famous 1886 story *The Death of Ivan Ilyich*. Ivan Ilyich's lifelong pursuit of social approval has won him only an unfulfilling career, an unhappy marriage, a distant relationship with his children, and a few rather shallow friendships. He is dying of some medical condition that the doctors are unable to diagnose. He himself doesn't want to accept this, and tries to push it out of his mind by focusing on his career, seeing friends, or even doing odd jobs at home like rearranging his bookshelves. His family also refuse to face it, his wife spending time seeking new medical treatments and pretending that they are working. When news of his death finally comes, again, no one seems to squarely face it. His colleagues think about who will get the promotion that his departure opens, his wife seeks financial advice to try and get tax benefits from his death, and his family fuss over the logistics of organizing a funeral and accommodating relatives from the provinces. Tolstoy is making the point that by all this busyness, no one is actually facing up to the sheer fact that this man is dead, and that one day, they too will all die.[3]

We saw in chapter 1 that Ernest Becker described this behavior as "the denial of death." This isn't simply an idea that occurs to therapists or novelists, but rather, Becker claims, is one of the most prevalent characteristics of the human race. We humans alone are fully aware of our own future death and can reflect upon it, he argued, but we don't easily come to terms with it. So, in order to avoid death as individuals we fill our lives with entertainment and distractions (such as drink, drugs, sex, and shopping), and as a society we create "hero-systems."[4] These are ways to make ourselves seem heroic, useful to creation, and to create a legacy that will outlast us: by building an empire, a temple, a totem pole, a skyscraper, a business, or a family that spans three generations. These will ensure that we are remembered after we have died—but

---

3. Tolstoy, *Death of Ivan Ilyich*.
4. Becker, *Denial of Death*, 5.

are also the source of much of the violence, tyranny, and sadness that the human race has faced, Becker argues.

However, Becker doesn't judge or look down on people for denying death. Facing death is grim and demanding, as the writings of the French philosopher Jean-Paul Sartre testify. Sartre was part of a group of thinkers called the existentialists, who took atheism and death really seriously. Sartre himself admired Tolstoy's story about Ivan Ilyich. "Atheism is a cruel long-term business, and I have gone through it to the end,"[5] Sartre said. He was such an influential philosopher in part because he conveyed his ideas through novels—in fact, he was awarded a Nobel Prize for Literature (but turned it down). His most famous novel, *Nausea,* sums up his central concerns. It is about Antoine Roquentin, a historian who is trying to write a book but is just too weighed down by the meaninglessness of life to make significant progress. At times reality melts away from him, at other times it overwhelms him. Roquentin is really the voice for Sartre's own thinking, musing that:

> I had appeared by chance, I existed like a stone, a plant, a microbe. I could feel nothing to myself but an inconsequential buzzing. I was thinking . . . that here we are eating and drinking, to preserve our precious existence, and that there's nothing, nothing, absolutely no reason for existing.

The climax of the book is when Roquentin is sitting on a park bench, and concludes that everything is superfluous, or unnecessary. When this realisation dawns, he contemplates but quickly dismisses suicide:

> I dreamed vaguely of killing myself, to destroy at least one of these superfluous existences. But my death itself would have been superfluous. Superfluous, my corpse, my blood on these pebbles, between these plants, in the depths of this charming park. And the decomposed flesh would have been superfluous in the earth which would have received it, and my bones, finally, cleaned, stripped,

5. Sartre, *Words,* 157.

neat and clean as teeth, would also have been superfluous; I was superfluous for all time.[6]

This is very dark, and the reader wonders how Roquentin will
extricate himself from it. Right at the end, we find out: Roquentin
decides to write a book, that is, this book, *Nausea*, even though he
knows it is superfluous. Even Sartre, ironically, is denying death.

So, most people avoid and deny death, and atheism is unable
to help us practically because for atheism death is just an absurd end
to a life that has no intrinsic meaning. That is partly why we struggle
to deal with crises like pandemics and wars, because they force us to
confront death. Can Christianity offer anything more positive? The
Bible helps us do three things: put death in its proper perspective,
live life well in the face of death, and know what follows it.

Putting Death in Its Proper Perspective

The first important Christian reflection on death is not to deny or
avoid it, but to put it in its proper place. As he draws close to his
own death, Ivan Ilyich, in Tolstoy's novel, exclaims, "Something
is wrong!" with a world where life ends in death.[7] The Bible has
a lot to say about death, and it affirms Ilyich's hunch that the very
existence of death in our world is not simply a blind fact of the universe, but actually an indication that something has gone wrong.

As we saw in chapter 3, death is absent from the Bible's account of *creation* in the early chapters of Genesis. Some people see
Eden as figurative and others as literal, but however we interpret it
the Genesis account is marked by an absence of death: no murder,
no disease, no war. It is perhaps hard for us to imagine, but Genesis
implies that these were not meant to be part of the human experience of life on earth. According to this narrative, death entered
our history due to what theologians call the fall—the sin of disobedience to God by our first parents, Adam and Eve, which had
profound consequences for them and us. Paul writes in his letter

---

6. Sartre, *Nausea*, 184–85.
7. Tolstoy, *Death of Ivan Ilyich*, 202.

to the church in Rome, "Therefore, just as sin entered the world through one man, and death through sin, so also death was passed on to all men, because all sinned."[8]

The Bible traces the story of death from this beginning with what the apostle Paul, in the New Testament, calls the "first Adam," to the death and resurrection of Jesus, whom he calls the "last Adam."[9] In this narrative, because of the cross, we have *redemption* and delivery from death. As the Letter to the Hebrews puts it: Jesus "suffered death so that by the grace of God he may taste death for everyone."[10] Jesus' death took the penalty of our sins, and his resurrection shows death's power is broken. Paul so exults in this that in his letter to the Corinthians he almost seems to taunt death: "Where, O death, is your victory? Where, O death, is your sting?!"[11] And finally, the Bible's narrative continues, death will be ended at the *restoration* of all things when Jesus returns at the close of time to remake heaven and earth. Seeing a vision of this in the book of Revelation, John hears a voice from God's throne calling out that, "There will be no more death or mourning or crying or pain, for the old order of things has passed away."[12]

So how can we summarize the Bible's perspective on death? In one word: as an *intruder*. During the early days of the 2020 COVID-19 lockdown I was in a Zoom videoconferencing meeting with a student and some colleagues. Suddenly, an unknown face flashed up, as an uninvited stranger popped onto our screens. There was confusion and disruption all round, until I found the button to remove him. I worked out later that I had actually inadvertently given him the code to the meeting. In a way, that's what death is to our world and our lives. It is an unwelcome intruder, whom we as a race have inadvertently invited into our lives. We must never downplay its importance, as it wreaks such havoc and sorrow. Jesus didn't downplay it—as we saw in the previous chapter, he himself

8. Rom 5:12.
9. 1 Cor 15:45.
10. Heb 2:9.
11. 1 Cor 15:55.
12. Rev 21:4.

wept at the death of his friend Lazarus, even though he was about to perform a miracle and raise him from the dead. But it is important to remember that death is still an intruder, who was disarmed at Calvary and who will finally be excluded from the human story forever when Jesus Christ returns to remake and restore creation.

Facing Death

Putting death in its right perspective allows us, secondly, to live well as we face—rather than avoid—it. In his famous 2005 commencement (graduation) address to Stanford University students, the late CEO of Apple Inc., Steve Jobs, said that, "Remembering that I'll be dead soon is the most important tool I've ever encountered to help me make the big choices in life."[13] This is a constant refrain in the Bible: "Teach us to number our days aright, that we may gain a heart of wisdom," prays the psalmist.[14] To remember that our days are numbered—that is, that we are going to die—is a valuable way to help us live wisely and use our precious time well. It also helps us deal with and make sense of death as we face it as a society.

For English people, 1966 is remembered (even for people like me who had not yet then been born) as the year in which "we" won the soccer world cup. But for the Welsh it is recalled for one of the darkest days in their nation's modern history. At 9:15am on Friday, 21st October, the last day before school holidays, there was a catastrophic collapse of a colliery slag heap just above the village of Aberfan. 40,000 cubic meters of coal slurry slid down the hill, engulfing Pantglas Junior school. One hundred and sixteen children and twenty-eight adults were killed. It was said that no one smiled for a year after that in Aberfan.

Dr. Martyn Lloyd-Jones, Minister of London's Westminster Chapel, but from Wales and who knew the village himself, was asked to preach at the first anniversary of the disaster in 1967. He chose for his text the words of Romans 8:23, "For I reckon that

13. Jobs, "You've Got to Find What You Love," para. 18.
14. Ps 90:12.

the sufferings of this present time are not worthy to be compared with the glory which shall be revealed in us." He spoke of how the future promise of restoration and eternal life provides consolation in our grief. Someone who was present later wrote to Lloyd-Jones and said:

> through your messages . . . we have all received, not only a wonderful blessing, but renewed courage and determination. After the services I saw mothers, who had lost little ones, and fathers also, smile with renewed hope in their faces.[15]

It would be hard to imagine what comfort an atheist perspective could have given to match that.

As well as helping us as a society to reflect on and find a way through great crises like Aberfan, a war, or a pandemic, the Bible's account of death can help each and every one of us as we face death personally. We can see that more clearly by contrasting a number of deathbed testimonies.

Ilyich exclaimed on his death-bed, "So what's it all about? What's it for? It's impossible. It can't really be true that life is so pointless and nasty! And if it really is so nasty and so pointless, then why must I die, and die suffering?"[16] For Ilyich, facing death was a bitter, lonely, and frightening experience. Ilyich is of course a fictional character, but much the same can be seen in the lives of real people. Svetlana Alliluyeva was the daughter of Soviet leader Josef Stalin. Stalin was responsible for the deaths of tens of millions of his own citizens as he forced his ruthless brand of atheistic communism on the Soviet peoples. Svetlana reported that, on his deathbed: "He suddenly lifted his left hand as though he were pointing to something above and bringing down a curse on us all. The gesture was incomprehensible and full of menace."[17] Svetlana herself came to embrace the Christian faith in exile.

---

15. Murray, *David Martin Lloyd-Jones*, 571–72.

16. Tolstoy, *Death of Ivan Ilyich*, 202.

17. Townend, "Last Days of Stalin," para. 2.

In contrast, the annals of Christianity are full of people facing death with hope and joy, because of their faith that it will unite them to Jesus forever. When John Wesley, the founder of Methodism, died in 1791, his nurse, Eliza Ritchie, recorded a moving description of his last words. Struggling to make himself heard, she records, and "finding we could not understand what he said, he paused a little, and then with all the remaining strength he had, cried out, 'The best of all is, God is with us.'"[18] More recently, David Watson, the minister of a church in York, died of cancer in 1984. In the months before his death, he wrote a book about his hope in Jesus and how this helped him:

> When I die, it is my firm conviction that I shall be more alive than ever, experiencing the full reality of all that God has prepared for us in Christ . . . The actual moment of dying is still shrouded in mystery, but as I keep my eyes on Jesus I am not afraid. Jesus has already been through death for us, and will be with us when we walk through it ourselves.[19]

For the Christian, although we may suffer and fear the pain involved, and although no one is spared the grief of losing loved ones, there is no need to avoid thinking about or fearing death in any fundamental sense. This is because we know that God is with us, and that death is the doorway into a life that is more real and vivid even than that which we now experience. We know that we will see our loved ones who have trusted in the Lord again, and that because Jesus is with us we will not be alone as we die: "Yea, though I walk in the valley of the shadow of death, I will fear no evil, for thou art with me," as Psalm 23 puts it in the beautiful words of the King James translation of the Bible.

18. Parker, *Journal of John Wesley*, 419.
19. Watson, *Fear No Evil*, 168.

Beyond the Grave: Judgment

In December 2012, friends and relatives of Chet Fitch, of Oregon, received Christmas cards from him. That might not sound surprising, because they received them from him every Christmas. This year it was remarkable, however, because he had died a few months earlier aged 88. It transpired that Chet, a lifelong practical joker, had hatched a plot with his barber who would send signed cards from Chet the Christmas after he died. Chet updated the mailing list over a number of years and gave him money for postage as the costs went up. "Heaven" was reported as the return address. Some cards said things like, "Unfortunately you won't be joining me here," or "I'll probably be seeing you (some sooner than you think)."[20]

Chet Fitch's humor actually underlines a claim that is repeated in different ways throughout the Bible: that "people are destined to die once, and after that to face judgment."[21] Throughout the Bible, the existence of the human personality beyond death is repeatedly affirmed. As the Bible proceeds it unfolds the claim that there are two destinations after death and judgment: a blissful presence of God, and a terrible separation from him (we call these heaven and hell, but the Bible uses various terms for them).[22] The third and final way that the Bible helps us to face death, therefore, is by telling us what comes after it.

We have already seen that the idea of heaven, or rather, as the Bible puts it, a new, remade heaven and earth, is a world where suffering and death are eliminated and where human relationships with each other, creation, and God himself are restored. We instinctively like that idea, but do not like idea of hell. "How can a loving God hate people enough to send them to hell?" we might ask.

It is not true that biblical teaching on judgment means that God hates anyone. The apostle Peter writes that God "is patient with you, not wanting anyone to perish, but everyone to come to

20. "Christmas Cards from Beyond the Grave," 30.
21. Heb 9:27.
22. Milne, *Message of Heaven and Hell*, 15–16.

repentance."[23] In the Old Testament, God says through the prophet Ezekiel that "I have no pleasure in the death of the wicked, but that the wicked turn from his way and live."[24] In Jesus' death, where he took the punishment our sins deserve, a loving God has provided a way out. No one needs be lost.

God's punishment is based on a just, controlled, reasonable hostility to all that is wrong and which mars his good creation. We know something of that ourselves. In 2010, a city I know and love, Osh, by the Kyrgyzstan-Uzbekistan boundary, was subject to horrendous ethnic-based violence between the majority Kyrgyz and minority Uzbek ethnic groups. There was blame on both sides, but the Uzbeks suffered disproportionately. Over 400 people were killed in three days of chaos marked by mass rape, looting, and arson. In the aftermath, criminal gangs and the police subjected the Uzbek minority to systematic robbery, false detention, and torture. Friends of mine were killed, robbed, or injured in a catastrophe that threatened to escalate into a regional crisis.[25] I visited soon afterwards, speaking to survivors as well as those who justified what had happened. As I walked around the once-vibrant, but now-ruined, neighborhoods that I knew so well, I felt sorrow, yes, but also anger: *This cannot stand! Justice must be done! The guilty must be made to answer for their crimes!* At such catastrophic moments we crave judgment: not petty revenge or hot-blooded retaliation, but an impartial judge to ensure that justice is done for the weak and vulnerable. We don't want sexual abusers of young women like Jimmy Saville in the UK or Jeffrey Epstein in the USA, or genocidal tyrants like Yugoslavia's Slobodan Milosevic or Uganda's Idi Amin, to cheat justice by their deaths. The Bible's message is that they won't—they will face their Creator as Judge at the end of time. And so will we.

Ultimately, the punishment of hell is a sovereign God upholding justice in the universe in respect of the choices that we as responsible beings make—even if those choices are disobedience

23. 2 Pet 3:9.

24. Ezek 33:11.

25. Megoran, *Nationalism in Central Asia*, ch. 4.

to him. Those choices have consequences for other people and for us before and after death. To live wisely is not to deny and avoid death, nor to pass selfish and unjust lives because we think that what we do doesn't ultimately matter if we can get away with it. Rather, knowing that we will stand before our maker at the end of our lives, to live wisely is to face death and remember that there will be eternal consequences of how we live. Instead of worrying about death, or ignoring it, or denying it through destructive behavior, we can actually look forward to it; and in the meantime we can commit ourselves to live meaningful lives marked by love of God and other people, knowing that nothing we do for good is in vain.

Evidence?

I once heard Chris Patten, former UK Chancellor of the Exchequer and then Chancellor of Newcastle University, quip in a graduation (commencement) address to my geography students that "The House of Lords [the UK's upper, nonelected parliamentary chamber] proves that there is life after death!" His joke raises a serious point: What is the evidence that all this is true? I once heard an atheist say that atheists need to accept that there is nothing they can offer to match the hope of the Christian doctrine of eternal life; what matters, he said, was whether that belief is true or not (he didn't think it was). This is, of course, absolutely right. The Christian belief in life after death is of staggering significance. It is a great comfort as we face death personally, or as we are confronted by it in a national or global crisis. It is a consolation for the grieving, knowing that they will see loved ones again. It is a solace for the oppressed, certain that the oppressors will ultimately answer for their actions. It is an inspiration for all those working for peace and justice, assured that their actions do matter. It is a motivation for scientists seeking to understand and cure deadly diseases, convinced that the Creator is pleased with their efforts. It is a source of great psychological and mental well-being, liberating us from the destructive behaviors that Ernest Becker identified as the "denial of death." And it is a warning to the powerful who think they can act with impunity because they believe that they can cheat justice by death.

So, the Christian teaching on life beyond death is of enormous personal and social value in helping us live well. But, in a sense, that is irrelevant: the most important question about it is: Is it *true*? If it isn't true, then it is simply a delusion and no honest human being wants to live out something that may not be real. How do we know what happens after we die? This question is raised by a "Harpers Song" inscribed in the tomb of the ancient Egyptian pharaoh Intef I, who ruled towards the end of the third millennium BC. Played by harpists during funeral feasts for the deceased, the song says of the afterlife:

> None comes from there,
> To tell of their needs,
> To calm our hearts,
> Until we go where they have gone.[26]

The unknown harpist is right: that is exactly the evidence we need, someone who comes back "from there" to tell us what it is like. The Bible's claim is that, 2,000 years after that song was written, someone actually *did* come back from the dead—Jesus.

We know of Jesus' resurrection from the eyewitness accounts recorded in the New Testament. We saw in chapter 2 that the reliability of the New Testament texts is unparalleled compared with anything else we have from antiquity. A primary focus of the New Testament is the resurrection of Jesus, claiming that it was witnessed by his closest friends and hundreds of people. It is hard to imagine that his disciples made this up. After Jesus' death they could have easily and safely melted away and returned to their previous occupations, most of them having been fishermen. Instead, they devoted their entire lives and all their energies to propagating not a set of moral teachings, but the claim that Jesus was alive and the Savior of all. They suffered great inconvenience and hardship for this, and many of them were killed. Why would they do that if they had made it up? It is far more likely that what they described

---

26. Ancient Egypt Online, "'Song of the Harper," lines 16–19.

is true. And if it is true that Jesus rose from the dead, we are able to learn about the afterlife from him.

Between 1961 and 1991, Robben Island, in the Atlantic Ocean, eleven kilometers off the South African coast, served as a maximum-security detention center for political prisoners of the Apartheid regime. It is now a World Heritage Site museum. I have never visited in person, but recently went on a virtual museum tour. Although I knew the history, just looking at the empty and eerily quiet exercise yards, cells, and watchtowers made it difficult to visualize what life was like for prisoners, hard to imagine that this peaceful place really was a place of such suffering and oppression. To help, the virtual tour was narrated by Vusumsi Mcongo, who was himself a former political prisoner there. He explained, for example, how the prisoners were forced to undertake long hours of hard labor in the island's quarries and, because they were not given sunglasses, many suffered irreparable damage to their vision in the blinding sunlight. He spoke with authority: he had been there and could tell us about it.[27]

Likewise, Daniel Clark says that when it comes to what happens to us after death, Jesus "speaks as an authoritative guide."[28] I am going ahead "to prepare a place for you,"[29] Jesus told his disciples before his death. Jesus' resurrection body shows us something of the life after death that awaits us. He still had wound marks on his hands and side, and was recognizable to his friends. According to the gospel accounts, he could talk and eat and touch and walk as before, but he could also now appear and disappear in a new way. Paul writes in his first letter to the church at Corinth that "For as in Adam all die, so in Christ all will be made alive."[30] We can face death with peace and certainty, knowing that Jesus Christ has gone on before us and is awaiting us there. We know that it is not the end, and that war, terrorism, tyranny, pandemics, or any other crisis that threatens to take our lives will not be the end of our stories.

27. "Robben Island Prison Tour."

28. Clark, *Dead or Alive?*, 52.

29. John 14:3.

30. 1 Cor 15:22.

Living towards Death

Manchester United star George Best was regarded as one of the best football players of the twentieth century. At the height of his prowess in the 1960s he helped his team lift five trophies in just four years. He died in 2005, only hours after his doctors issued a statement saying, "His hours are numbered."[31] However, the truth is that his hours were numbered from the day that he was born, and if he had recovered in 2005 they would still have been numbered. He would have died at a later point.

The realization of this can suddenly burst in on us. The Chinese-American geographer, Yi-Fu Tuan, recalls what he describes as "the nightmarish logic with which my own mortality was first impressed on me." When he was twelve years old he had a nightmare that he was going to die. Relief came when he woke and found it was only a dream: but that relief passed quickly as he realized that because he was indeed alive "the awful consequence—death—therefore remained."[32] He actually *was* going to die someday! And so are we. Like George Best, our days are numbered, but unlike Yi-Fu Tuan, many of us have never really accepted the reality. A national or global crisis or catastrophe makes it harder for us not to accept that reality.

The question we face then is: How do we live with the reality of death? Do we let it frighten and terrify us? That is debilitating and depressive. Do we avoid it and forget about it? Many people do try that, but that is simply burying our heads in the sand and can lead to many destructive problems in the way that we live. It is also something that we can never truly avoid: death always catches up with us. Or can we allow this insight to help us live better, more healthily and joyfully, as we number our days aright and approach death without fear?

Atheism cannot help us here. Sartre, in *Nausea*, wrote, "Every [living thing] is born without reason, prolongs itself out

---

31. "George Best's 'Hours Are Numbered.'"
32. Tuan, *Who Am I?*, 95.

of weakness and dies by chance."[33] Bertrand Russell, one of the twentieth century's leading atheist thinkers, thought ahead in his autobiography to his eventual death. He described that moment as the "night of nothingness." He notes, "There is darkness without, and when I die there will be darkness within. There is no splendour, no vastness anywhere; only triviality for a moment, and then nothing." He concludes this grim reflection by asking, "Why live in such a world? Why even die?"[34]

That is very bleak. Russell admitted that as he got older he lost any sense of life having purpose and value, and death was simply the ultimate summary of that futility. How different are the words of the apostle Paul. Like Russell, he looked with anticipation toward the moment of his own death. He said, in contrast, "To me, to live is Christ, to die is gain."[35] As we have seen in this chapter, Christianity puts death in its proper perspective, helps us live well in facing it, and points to what happens afterwards. Because of this Paul actually looked forward to life after his death, and in the meantime lived intensely and authentically not in spite of that future, but because of it—it gave meaning and color and purpose to the present.

In an age of financial crises, wars, pandemics, and tyranny, could it be that in St. Paul, rather than Bertrand Russell, we have a better guide to facing death well?

---

33. Sartre, *Nausea*, 191.

34. Russell, *Autobiography of Bertrand Russell*, 159.

35. Phil 1:21, 23.

5

How Can We Live Well during a Global Crisis?[1]

THE SECOND WORLD WAR and its mass killing of Jews and others by Nazi Germany was among the worst crises that humanity has ever experienced. One of the more striking survivor's accounts to emerge was that of Corrie ten Boom, a Dutch Christian sent with her sister, Betsie, to the Ravensbrück concentration camp as punishment for sheltering Jews from the occupying forces. In the camp, Betsie and Corrie didn't abandon hope, but rather cared for and encouraged other prisoners, sharing God's love and joy with them. Betsie died in Ravensbrück, but after the war Corrie spent her life speaking and writing and helping others experiencing crises of their own. She even met and forgave one of the camp jailers after the war. Corrie made this striking statement:

> It is not as much what happens, but *how we take it* that is important. God is watching to see whether we allow the problems to defeat us, or whether we will go through

1. Parts of this chapter were first presented in Newcastle University's Insights online public lecture series, in a June 2011 address entitled, "What's the Point of University during a Pandemic? Hints from C. S. Lewis and J. R. R. Tolkien."

them in His strength, being made stronger for the next problem and ultimately for the final end battle."[2]

As Corrie Ten Boom observes, how we respond to crises matters a great deal. That was the lesson from academic research about responses to March 2020 COVID-19 lockdowns. Two main responses were identified. *Acceptors* tended to accept the situation and were not observing noticeable effects on their sleep, whereas *sufferers* were struggling with the lockdown, being anxious and losing sleep.[3] The report highlighted the unsurprising finding that different people cope and respond differently to the same crisis. This book has so far considered some of the big philosophical and religious questions raised by the pandemic, but in this final chapter it switches to the more practical question about how we can live well in these times. What practical use is Christianity in a crisis?

In this final chapter I outline six *practices* of the Christian life that can enable us to live well in uncertain and dangerous times. These are illustrated by the lives of Christian people during crises over many centuries and down to our own age.

Worshiping

Worshiping is a Christian practice that helps us live well during a crisis. It is the emotional expression of adoration of God. Psalm 103 (a poem recorded in the Bible) says let "everything within me praise his holy name." Worship is a whole life lived in admiration of God, a focus that molds our values and responses to personal, community, or global crises.

Worship might seem bizarre, even demeaning, in our democratic age. Why does God need to be worshiped, we might ask? As atheist Stephen Fry put it, God must be "totally selfish" if he demands that "We have to spend our life on our knees thanking him."[4] This misses the point: worship is what we do when we direct

---

2. Rosewell, *Five Silent Years,* 109 (italics original).

3. Duffy and Allington, "Three Ways People Are Reacting to Coronavirus."

4. Perry, "Stephen Fry Says," para. 7.

our energies and set our value and affections on something greater than us and our circumstances. Humans cannot avoid worshiping. Novelist and atheist David Wallace highlighted this in his startlingly honest 2005 commencement speech to students of Kenyon College:

> In the day-to-day trenches of adult life, there is actually no such thing as atheism. There is no such thing as not worshipping. Everybody worships. The only choice we get is *what* to worship. And an outstanding reason for choosing some sort of God or spiritual-type thing to worship . . . is that pretty much anything else you worship will eat you alive. If you worship money and things—if they are where you tap real meaning in life—then you will never have enough . . . Worship your own body and beauty and sexual allure and you will always feel ugly, and when time and age start showing, you will die a million deaths before they finally plant you . . . Worship power—you will feel weak and afraid, and you will need ever more power over others to keep the fear at bay. Worship your intellect, being seen as smart—you will end up feeling stupid, a fraud, always on the verge of being found out. And so on. [5]

A crisis like a war or pandemic stops us doing so many things. If we worship those things—that is to say if they are what we live for and where we get our value and self-esteem from—then we will struggle. Those things may be the work we do, the career opportunities we have lost, the leisure and travel we had planned, the people we wanted to see, our bodily comfort. If those are what we worship, when they get taken from us we will struggle and be frustrated or afraid.

In the Bible, the book the Acts of the Apostles tells the story of one of the earliest leaders of the Christian church, the apostle Paul. He went with his co-worker Silas to the city of Philippi and started a church there, but local businesses thought that Paul and Silas were harming their money-making opportunities and so stirred up a mob against them. The pair were set upon, dragged through the streets, stripped and beaten, and then the magistrates

5. Wallace. *This Is Water,* 98–111 (italics original).

ordered them to be severely flogged, thrown into jail, and fastened in the stocks. Imprisoned, suffering and in pain, they faced a possible death by mob lynching or execution.

Yet, the Bible's narrative continues, "About midnight Paul and Silas were praying and singing hymns to God."[6] This is remarkable. Referring to this account, Martyn Lloyd-Jones writes that "Christianity is the most practical thing in the world today," because it enables people to sing in prison.[7] It was because Paul and Silas worshiped Jesus Christ—not success, comfort, their work, career, or even their lives—that they could worship and sing in prison. Paul had to leave Philippi after this mob attack, and later wrote a letter to the church there: "I know what it is to be in need, and I know what it is to have plenty. I have learned the secret of being content in any and every situation,"[8] he said. That secret is worship, which sets us free to deal with whatever life throws at us. It is not that worship stops us suffering or makes us deny it or pretend that it isn't there. Rather, it stops us being crushed because our hope, pleasure, and joy is in the eternal God, not in the circumstances that—as we have found with recent pandemics, wars, or financial collapses—can change dramatically and quickly.

Seeing

The study about different reactions to the Coronavirus lockdown found that one of the big differences between "accepters" and "sufferers" was that sufferers were much more likely to look at social media. We can easily lose a sense of perspective, and get scared and angry. The Christian practice of *seeing the bigger picture* of eternity is helpful in maintaining a sense of perspective, and as an example of this I look to C. S. Lewis.

In October 1939, one month after Britain declared war on Germany, Lewis delivered a sermon to Oxford University students

6. Acts 16:25.

7. Lloyd-Jones, *I Am Not Ashamed,* 31.

8. Phil 4:12.

later published as the essay "Learning in War-Time." He began by observing what an odd thing it was for them to be studying at that time in history. Your studies may be disrupted by war and military service, he told the students, but even if not, he asked them, "How can we continue to take an interest in these placid occupations when the lives of our friends and the liberties of Europe are in the balance?" Referring to the legend that the Roman emperor Nero played a fiddle while the empire's capital was on fire, he asked, "Is it not like fiddling while Rome burns?"[9]

That question resonates with us during crises like the CO-VID-19 pandemic. Instead of the daily news reporting the latest football results and cricket scores, the pandemic gave us a macabre list of new infections and deaths at home and around the world. Economic and social life was turned upside down. People in the health and emergency services were lauded during the initial phases of the lockdown as "key workers." What about the rest of us, doing apparently less important, even trivial things (like teaching geography online, perhaps)? Is this not also "fiddling while Rome burns?"

Lewis gave a striking answer to his own question "to a Christian the true tragedy of Nero must be not that he fiddles while the city was on fire but that he fiddles on the brink of hell."[10] Given eternal destinies, how can we justify spending even a fraction of our time on things that are comparatively trivial? Lewis answered that we are mistaken to compare a situation like the war with normal life, because life has never been normal or secure. We must not allow the crisis at hand to absorb all our attention, worry and concern. God alone demands that we surrender our all to him. But this is not at the expense of everything else: Christianity in no way excludes all the ordinary activities of life—rather, we do these before God. As Paul wrote to the Corinthians, "So whether you eat or drink or whatever you do, do it all for the glory of God."[11]

9. Lewis, "Learning in War-Time," 26.

10. Lewis, "Learning in War-Time," 26.

11. 1 Cor 10:31.

For Lewis, this perspective afforded some very practical advice about living in a crisis like the Second World War. Don't get overobsessed or stressed (something that endlessly trawling through social media makes far more likely). Don't get frustrated at being unable to achieve all you want to. And don't give in to fear. The war, he said, doesn't increase our chances of dying—they remain exactly 100 percent—but war makes death more real to us. He elaborated that "The war creates no absolutely new situation: it simply aggravates the permanent human situation so that we can no longer ignore it."[12] Finally, Lewis advised his listeners to continue in whatever they were doing beforehand, if they believed that this was their calling from God at this point in their lives. Don't let something like a world war distract you from the more important issues of living life in the light of our eternal destiny, he warned. Lewis was not being naïve about the war, here—after all, he had endured and been injured in the horrors of trench warfare in World War One.

We can draw parallels with our time of pandemic and wars, when death is close and the future seems uncertain. As Christians, we know that death and then an eternal destiny await us all. Let us not so fill our minds with the current crisis that we become so stressed, frustrated, or afraid that we lose sight of God and suffer mental turmoil. The Christian practice of seeing time in the light of eternity allows us to pray, "Give us this day our daily bread," and live one day at a time in humble and joyful obedience to him.

Lamenting

On March 16, 1985, Associated Press journalist Terry Anderson was seized in Beirut by the Islamic Jihad terror group. He was held in captivity for nearly seven years, longer than any of the other Westerners taken hostage in Lebanon during the 1980s. It was obviously a terrible ordeal, with Anderson subject to daily humiliation by his captors and not knowing whether he would be released

---

12. Lewis, "Learning in War-Time," 27.

or executed. His partner, Madeleine, was pregnant at the time of his abduction, and he would not meet his daughter until she was six years old. Although most of us will never experience anything as extreme as this, feelings of isolation, powerlessness, fear, and separation from loved ones are perhaps recognizable to us as we or our communities face the effects of economic collapse, war and terrorism, or pandemic lockdowns. In the same way, we can learn from Anderson the value of a third Christian practice for living well during a global crisis: *lamenting*, which is the pouring out to God of passionate grief, disappointment, regret, and sadness.

Before his captivity, Terry had been on a journey of faith as he rediscovered the Christian background he had been brought up in. Allowed a Bible in captivity, he devoured its contents, finding the voices of Paul and the Old Testament prophets coming "completely alive."[13] But what spoke to him most were the songs and poems of lament, particularly in the Old Testament books of Job and the Psalms. Job is a study of a successful man leading an apparently charmed life who suddenly and (to him) inexplicably suffers a series of catastrophic tragedies, from the deaths of his children to the loss of his health and wealth. Anderson said that, during captivity, he "studied and studied Job" and although he could not always understand it, he found that "suddenly parts of it sound as if I could have written them,"[14] such as chapter 7 verse 3:

> . . . I am allotted months of futility,
> and nights of misery are appointed me.
> When I lie down I think: 'When will I get up?'
> But the night drags on,
> and I toss and turn until dawn.

Using Psalm 13 as an example, Anderson wrote that, "The psalms contain verse after verse that speak directly to me, and about me, in beautiful, clear phrases":

> How long, Lord? Will you forget me forever?
> How long will you hide your face from me?

13. Anderson, *Den of Lions*, 125.

14. Anderson, *Den of Lions*, 125.

How long must I wrestle with my thoughts
    and day after day have sorrow in my heart?
How long will my enemy triumph over me? Look on me and
answer, Lord my God.[15]

These poems of lament, or songs of "disorientation," as theologian Walter Bruggeman termed them,[16] allow us to give voice to deep anguish, confusion, sorrow, and anger when life doesn't work out as we would like it to, and when we cannot find neat and tidy answers to the big questions that assail us. Lamenting is a thoroughly and authentically Christian response to such experiences. It is important that we turn our hearts and minds to reflect on issues of meaning and purpose. It is helpful to consider suffering and death and be assured that it is all not simply futile and meaningless. It is right to help those in need by practically assisting them, providing comfort for them, and sharing with them the eternal message of the gospel. But it is vital that this is never at the cost of minimizing or trivializing our pain. Paul says, in the Bible, "weep with those who weep"[17]—not "cheer them up" or "provide them with some easy answers to show them why they shouldn't be weeping."

There is much to lament during crises like the pandemic, the global financial crisis, terrorism, or war—sickness, bereavement, death, isolation, separation, fear, unemployment, bankruptcy, poverty, poor public health responses, broken relationships, selfishness, and lost opportunities and futures. The modern world isn't good at lamenting. We may have (thankfully) abandoned the "stiff upper lip" attitude of a previous generation that discouraged any display of what was perceived to be emotional weakness. However, our culture too often ends up reveling in hopeless self-pity, lashing out in blind anger at the person whom we blame for causing or mismanaging a crisis, or thinking that we can sort out a problem through addressing it therapeutically. In contrast, lamenting is a biblical practice of expressing our deepest pain and fear and loss

15. Anderson, *Den of Lions*, 125.

16. Brueggemann, *Message of the Psalms*, 51–58.

17. Rom 12:15.

and anger in a passionate and heartfelt way, but expressing them before the God who is there, who made us, who loves us, and who hears and cares about our distress. Lamenting, and helping others with the vocabulary to lament, is a proper Christian way to live well during a personal or global crisis.

Helping

A fourth Christian practice for living well in a time of crisis is *helping* others, or "mercy." Between AD 249 and 262, a deadly pandemic began in Asia and afflicted Europe and Africa, wreaking havoc on the Roman Empire. Its pathology included fatigue, bloody stools, fever, vomiting, and severe infection, and survivors suffered debilitation, loss of hearing, and blindness. The pestilence was indiscriminate, invading "every house" as one contemporary put it, with a report on demographic consequences from the Bishop of Alexandria implying that the city's population had declined by about 62 percent (from something like 500,000 down to 190,000). No pestilence so destructive had been recorded previously in the empire. Historian Kyle Harper suggests it was most likely either a viral haemorrhagic fever or an influenza pandemic.[18]

Historians named the disease "The Cyprian Plague" after Cyprian, Bishop of Carthage, whose writings on it are one of the main contemporary historical sources available to us. Prior to the plague, Christians in Carthage had been subjected to what Pontius, in his *Life of Cyprian,* terms "an unusual and violent rage of a cruel persecution" that "laid waste God's people."[19] When the plague struck, those who could manage to (generally the rich) fled the city, but Cyprian urged the believers not to save themselves, but to remain in the city and care for those in need even though they had had been persecuting them. Cyprian said in a sermon that:

> there was nothing wonderful in our cherishing our own
> people only with the needed attentions of love, but that

18. Harper, *Fate of Rome,* ch. 4.
19. Pontius the Deacon, "Life and Passion of Cyprian," paras. 8–9.

he might become perfect who would do something more than the publican or the heathen, who, overcoming evil with good, and practicing a clemency which was like the divine clemency, loved even his enemies.

The believers remained, seeking to care for all in the city. This led to a growth in Christianity, as this demonstration of the love of Jesus won converts to the faith.

Cyprian's story, and the biblical practice of showing love to the needy by helping, has been repeated time and again down the ages. In 1527, bubonic plague reached the German town of Wittenberg, and the Elector of Saxony, John the Steadfast, ordered the reformer Martin Luther to leave. Rather than flee for safety, however, he stayed, with his pregnant wife Katharina. In a letter to a fellow pastor, Luther set out what he thought Christians (specifically pastors) should do "when a deadly epidemic strikes." Although he reasoned that it is not necessarily sinful to flee from danger, he made two main suggestions. First, remembering that "we are mutually bound together," pastors should "serve our neighbour" by attending to the needs of the sick and dying, "risking our lives in the manner as St John teaches, 'If Christ laid down his life for us, we ought to lay down our lives for the brethren.'"[20] Putting this into practice, the Luthers opened their house to the sick.

But this was not the sort of reckless disregard for public health that some people have advocated for moral or religious reasons during the COVID-19 pandemic. Luther described some people who were:

> much too rash and reckless, tempting God and disregarding everything which might counteract death and the plague. They disdain the use of medicines; they do not avoid places and persons infected by the plague, but lightheartedly make sport of it and wish to prove how independent they are.[21]

---

20. Luther, "Whether One May Flee," 119–38.
21. Luther, "Whether One May Flee," 131.

Although they may dress this up in religious language, "This is not trusting God but tempting him,"[22] because, Luther argued, "God has created medicines and provided us with intelligence to guard and take good care of the body."[23]

This historic Christian practice of helping the needy and suffering is an authentic way to live well during the COVID-19 pandemic, and has been demonstrated in creative ways by churches all over the world. This started in Wuhan, right where the pandemic itself began, with local Christians distributing scarce face masks to try and slow the outbreak as they shared the good news of the Christian message. One person involved in this blogged, "Christians gained the respect they never had because of their willingness to risk their health to serve."[24] This mirrored Cyprian's and Luther's experiences centuries earlier, and the response of Wuhan's Christians has inspired fellow believers around the world to take up this practice of helping as an authentic biblical response to a crisis like the pandemic.

Building Alternatives

A fifth Christian response to global or national crises is *building alternative communities*. In the previous chapter we met Kefa Sempangi, the Uganda lecturer in art history who set up a thriving church as a response to Idi Amin's increasingly corrupt and bloodthirsty reign. On Easter Sunday, 1973, he was confronted by five of Idi Amin's assassins. "We are going to kill you. If you have anything to say, say it before you die," the leader said, pointing a gun at him. Sempangi recounts what happened next:

> From far away I heard a voice, and I was astonished to realize that it was my own. "I do not need to plead my own cause," I heard myself saying. "I am a dead man already. My life is dead and hidden in Christ. It is your lives that

22. Luther, "Whether One May Flee," 131.
23. Luther, "Whether One May Flee," 131.
24. Lee, "Christians in Wuhan," para. 9.

are in danger, you are dead in your sins. I will pray to
God that after you have killed me, he will spare you from
eternal destruction.[25]

The leader lowered his weapon and ordered his men to do
likewise. Sempangi was so shocked when the leader asked him to
pray for them that he was "speechless,"[26] and the assassin had to re-
peat the request! Keeping his own eyes open in case it was a trick, he
prayed that God would save them from death. The leader promised
that he would protect him, and said, "I saw widows and orphans in
your congregation . . . I saw them singing and giving praise. Why
are they happy when death is so near?" Sempangi replied, "Because
they are loved by God," who "has given them life."[27]

This is not just a story of divine protection, but rather an example of a typically authentic Christian response to a crisis like
genocidal rule and unchecked violence: building alternatives.
Although a university lecturer, Sempangi devoted a lot of time
to leading the church he set up. Amin's rule was characterized
by shocking human rights abuses, extrajudicial killings, and oppression of opponents and ethnic minorities—up to half a million
people may have died under his regime. The church was a community of people who lived out a different reality in the midst of
this violence. Worshiping Jesus as Lord and King (rather than a
political leader like Idi Amin), and choosing to live by different
loyalties, the church is a community of people characterized by
peace, nonviolence, love, mutual care, communal sharing of resources, hope, and humility. As he told me in an interview, at the
time of Amin people flocked to the church "because there was so
much killing in the country, the only way people could find life
was in the church." Over time, Sempangi established the Presbyterian Church in Uganda which now has 250 congregations, sharing
the love and life of God that was such a witness and hope during
the dark days of Amin's terror.

25. Sempangi, *Reign of Terror*, 105–7.

26. Interview, Kefa Sempangi, Uganda, 07/05/2015. This account is a re-
working of one that appeared in Megoran, *Warlike Christians*, 227–29.

27. See Sempangi, *Reign of Terror*, 105–7.

Sempangi's authentic Christian response to the crisis that befell his country did not end there. Idi Amin was overthrown in 1979 following an invasion by neighboring Tanzania. The country was free of a tyrant, but devastated after years of misrule. Sempangi responded to this crisis by addressing both its consequences and causes. The violence which Uganda had witnessed had created vast numbers of orphans. These were children who in many cases had seen their parents brutally murdered in front of their eyes, and who now, on the streets, lived lives that were violent and twisted because of all they had witnessed. Sempangi established orphanages that cared for the hardest of children, providing them with love and future opportunities. These children have in many cases gone on to transform the communities in which they later came to live in, and to serve as pastors in the Presbyterian Church in Uganda. The practice of building alternative communities is a compelling Christian response to a crisis.

Hoping

In 1938, J. R. R. Tolkien penned a short story called "Leaf: by Niggle." Tolkien was, like his friend C. S. Lewis, a Christian, and this story illustrates the final Christian practice that can help us live well during a crisis—*hoping*.

The story begins like this:

> There was once a little man called Niggle, who had a long journey to make. He did not want to go, indeed the whole idea was distasteful to him; but he could not get out of it. He knew he would have to start some time, but he did not hurry with his preparations.[28]

As the story proceeds, we learn that Niggle is a painter. But "Not a very successful one," Tolkien writes, "partly because he had many other things to do. Most of these things he thought were a nuisance; but he did them fairly well, when he could not get out

28. Tolkien, "Leaf," 75.

of them: which (in his opinion) was far too often."[29] These niggles were things like "acquaintances" popping round for tea, but principally the frequent and annoying demands of a lazy neighbor called Parish.

Aware that a "journey" is about to take place, Niggle decides to focus on his great project—a tree, and the whole landscape behind it, on a vast canvas stretched out in his studio. But, because of the niggles, all he ever got done was the leaf. His last attempt to make a concerted effort to focus on the task is thwarted when Parish comes to tell Niggle that his roof is leaking and wife is ill, and to ask Niggle if he would cycle to town and call a doctor. He does so, catches cold, and then "the driver" comes to take him on "the journey," which is his death. The canvas is used to patch up Parish's roof, and a little bit only survives—the leaf, which is framed and displayed in the town's museum with the title, "Leaf: by Niggle." However eventually the museum burns down, and he is forgotten.

The story was devised just before World War Two. Tolkien was struggling to complete *The Lord of The Rings*, distracted by frustrating niggles and fearing the shadow that Nazism cast over Europe: Would he live to be able to complete his work? I am sure that we can all sympathize with Tolkien, and not just in a global crisis like a war. There is so much that we want to get done in life: so many people we want to be good friends and family to, places we'd like to see, charities and campaigns and communities we'd like to support, so many ways we would like to develop our health or character or skills or education. But niggles get in the way: bad health, unanticipated additional demands on our time, unexpected jobs around the house that need doing, exciting opportunities we can't turn down, helping other people, waiting half an hour on hold as we try to call the internet supplier about a disruption, etc. A national crisis can be "niggles on steroids": so many plans disrupted in so many ways, so many additional demands on us, so many ordinary activities made much harder.

But Tolkien's story continues. "The journey" eventually takes Niggle to a new land, which we come to understand as heaven.

29. Tolkien, "Leaf," 75.

As he walks through it he suddenly comes upon a tree, which he recognizes, astoundingly, as the tree that he had been working on but been unable to complete:

> Before him stood the Tree, his Tree, finished . . . a Tree that was alive, its leaves opening, its branches growing and bending in the wind that Niggle had so often felt or guessed, and had so often failed to catch . . . All the leaves he had ever laboured at were there, as he had imagined them . . . and there were others that had only budded in his mind, and many that might have budded, if only he had had time . . . they were just exquisite leaves.[30]

Tim Keller writes this, of the story: "maybe you went in to town planning with a vision about what a real city should look like—you are likely to be discouraged." Or perhaps you studied to become a lawyer, pursuing a vision for justice and a society ruled by peace and equity, You will get disillusioned because you will find out that as much as you are trying to work on important things, much of what you do is minutiae. "Once or twice in your life you may feel like you have finally 'gotten a leaf out.'" But:

> Whatever your work, you need to know this: There really is a tree. Whatever you are seeking in your work—the city of justice and peace, the world of brilliance and beauty, the story, the order, the healing—it is there . . . Your work will be only partially successful, on your best days, in bringing that world about. But inevitably the whole tree that you seek—the beauty, harmony, justice, comfort, joy, and community—will come to fruition.[31]

If we have no hope of everlasting life, then everything we do on earth is meaningless and not getting it done may simply compound this meaninglessness. What this story suggests, however, is that the hope of a new heavens and earth helps us deal with those frustrations. We can accept our limits and recognize that our work is always incomplete, but can rest assured that the good world we

---

30. Tolkien, "Leaf," 88–89.
31. Keller, *Every Good Endeavour,* 15.

strive towards will come to fruition in a new reality created by God himself. The Christian faith fills us with a hope that allows us to accept the unexpected restrictions or frustrations thrust on us, but at the same time to continue to live and work for the things that are important because we know they point towards the great reality of the work that God is doing on earth, and ultimately to the new heavens and earth. This is hoping, an integral Christian practice that helps us live well during a time of crisis.

Trusting God in a Global Crisis

In 1854, nineteen-year-old Charles Haddon Spurgeon arrived in London from rural Cambridgeshire to serve as pastor of the New Park Street chapel. In the same year, 10,000 Londoners were killed by a cholera pandemic that had originated in India. The outbreak struck most intensely in the neighborhood of New Park Street,[32] and it was an exceptionally demanding time for the highly gifted but still inexperienced young man, who recalled that, "Family after family summoned me to the bedside of the smitten, and almost every day I was called to visit the grave."[33] He wrote that "I gave myself up with youthful ardour to the visitation of the sick," but as his "friends seemed falling one by one" he was on the verge of exhaustion, feeling that, "my burden was heavier than I could bear." This could have broken the man and his ministry. However, God had other plans, and at this low point, returning home from a funeral, he was led by curiosity to read a handwritten sign in a shoemaker's window in the Dover Road. It quoted Psalm 91, verse 9, "Because thou hast made the Lord, which is my refuge, even the most High, thy habitation; there shall no evil befall thee, neither shall any plague come nigh thy dwelling."

Spurgeon wrote that "The effect upon my heart was immediate. Faith appropriated the passage as her own," and he felt refreshed and strengthened in his work, continuing with his visitation of the

32. Nettles, *Living by Revealed Truth*, 77.
33. Spurgeon, *Treasury of David*, 92.

dying in "a calm and peaceful spirit" and feeling "no fear of evil." He did not presume that this meant he was immune to disease—it was a respiratory viral infection, probably an influenza epidemic, that ended his life in 1892.[34] But in the meantime he would go on to pastor the congregation for almost four decades, transforming it into what might now be called the world's first megachurch, opening orphanages for the city's boys and girls who had lost parents due to disease or other causes, and exercising a global influence through his books and sermons which remain in print to this day. But he never forgot the lessons of that pandemic and how he could trust in God to give him the strength to continue living for him by serving and helping others.

Recent crises like the post-2001 wars and Islamist terrorism, the 2007–08 financial collapse, the COVID-19 pandemic, and the 2022 Russian invasion of Ukraine have many precedents in world history. By reading their Bibles, Christians have learnt ways to respond to them. The six practices that we have considered in this chapter of worshiping God, seeing the eternal perspective, lamenting the tragedy, loving and helping the sick and needy, building alternative realities (church communities), and hoping and trusting in God are tried and tested over centuries of history in the face of epidemics, wars, tyranny, persecution, financial collapses, and natural disasters. These practices do not make us immune from suffering, grief, sickness and death. But they do help us live well during a personal, national, or global crisis.

---

34. Nettles, *Living by Revealed Truth*, 633–34.

Conclusion

Answers in an Age of Global Crises?

IN APRIL AND MAY 2020, two well-known people were thrust by the COVID-19 pandemic into the media spotlight, but for two very different reasons. In the USA, Francis Collins was overseeing the country's scientific effort to create a vaccine for the virus, and in the UK, Hylton Murray-Philpson was nearly killed by it. What they both had in common was that their consideration of the big questions of life had led them to faith in Jesus Christ, and this faith proved of immense practical help at the time.

Francis Collins was the Director of the US National Institutes of Health. As we saw in chapter 2, he was formerly the lead scientist on the Human Genome Project and came to faith when, as he put it in a 2020 interview with *Time Magazine*, "I was trying to prove my atheism and discovered that atheism is probably the least rational of all the choices."[1] In May 2020, he was awarded the prestigious Templeton Prize for his work on demonstrating the harmony of science and religion. His Christian faith inspired and enabled his pursuit of science, and after learning of the award he told the media that his faith has informed his response to the pandemic. He said that although he has wondered why God allowed

1. Luscombe "Having an Effective Vaccine," para. 37.

the pandemic to happen, he was particularly fond of Psalm 46: "God is our refuge and strength, an ever-present help in trouble," and elaborated that this:

> makes it pretty clear, there is going to be trouble. But God is there as a very present help and as a refuge and a strength. If we want to look at God's role in the coronavirus pandemic, that's where I'd look.[2]

He added that as Christians "we have to have as our No. 1 priority that we are going to care for the sick and the vulnerable," saying that for him this meant "I'm spending 100 hours a week trying to make sure we're bringing every kind of idea, capability and resource toward finding treatment, vaccines and diagnostic tests."[3]

One month earlier, British newspapers published interviews with COVID-19 survivor, environmentalist Hylton Murray-Philipson. He had been very ill with the virus, spending ten days in intensive care. During this period his father had died, but he was unable to attend the funeral. "I drifted in and out of consciousness," he said later. "When I coughed I couldn't suck in breath because of the tube down my throat, so I started to panic. I had this sense of drowning and dying."[4] Murray-Philipson survived, and moving images of him being wheeled out of hospital applauded by the National Health Service staff who had helped save his life were widely reported and shared.

In subsequent interviews, he spoke of how his Christian faith helped him. "The story of Jesus calming the waters for his disciples on the Sea of Galilee appeared in my mind," he said. It comforted him not just to know Jesus was with him, but that he would be with him as he faced the possibility of death:

> After a while, I began to have doubts as to how much longer I could do this for because I was wiped out by my struggle for breath. I had flashbacks to all sorts of different times in my life. I have a strong faith and the

2. Post, "NIH Chief Francis Collins Wins Templeton Prize," para. 21.

3. Post, "NIH Chief Francis Collins Wins Templeton Prize," para. 4.

4. Johnson, "Coronavirus Survivor," para. 6.

idea of falling into the arms of a loving God became quite appealing. I would be able to rejoin my wife, who I love very much and who died four years ago.[5]

How could Francis Collins and Hylton Murray-Philipson say these things with such apparent certainty? It was because they believed that the Bible's answers to some of the big questions about life, God, suffering, death, and eternity were true. But this was not simply an intellectual assent to a set of answers. It was because those answers had led them into a personal relationship with the God who is alive and real. This did not mean that they claimed to have water-tight answers to all the big questions. As we saw, Collins freely shared that he did not know why God permitted the pandemic. But what this faith did do for both men was to provide peace and the confidence that Jesus was with them in a way that helped them practically when faced with this great crisis in their own lives and that of the world. For ultimately the Bible's answers to these big questions is not a set of statements about the world, but a Person—Jesus Christ, the Son of God who loves us and came among us to bear on the cross our sin and suffering and sorrow and make everlasting life possible.

Hylton Murray-Philipson believed that death would not mean his destruction, but rather that he would fall "into the arms of a loving God," a reference to a great biblical promise that "The eternal God is your refuge, and underneath are the everlasting arms."[6] If this promise is true, and if that God really did come to us in Jesus Christ, and if Jesus will return at the end of time to remake the world and bring a final end to death and suffering, then this is not only the greatest comfort we could know during hard times, but one of the most remarkable claims ever put before humanity. It is so remarkable that it at least demands our serious scrutiny before we dismiss it. I would not dare to assume that I have answered or could answer all the big questions thrown up by crises discussed in this book, like pandemics, tyrannical regimes, terrorism, war, and financial and industrial disasters. Nor would I presume that I

5. Johnson, "Coronavirus Survivor," para. 8.

6. Deut 33:27.

have been able to convince you that Jesus Christ is who he says he is. But I hope that reading this book has at least prompted you to think that his claims are worth taking seriously enough to explore them further.

Bibliography

Albeity, Heba. "Capturing Chinggis Qahan in the Secret History of Mongols." May 5, 2010. http://albeityacademic.blogspot.com/2010/05/capturing-chinggis-qahan-in-secret.html

Alexander, Denis. *Creation or Evolution: Do We Have to Choose?* London: Monarch, 2008.

———. *Rebuilding the Matrix: Science and Faith in the 21st Century*. Oxford: Lion, 2001.

Ancient Egypt Online. "Song of the Harper." https://ancientegyptonline.co.uk/harper-song/

Anderson, Terry. *Den of Lions: Memoirs of Seven Years in Captivity*. London: Hodder & Stoughton, 1994.

Ashcraft, Michael. "Pandemic Shuts Down Red Light Districts in India, Sex Workers Liberated." *God Reports* (June 29, 2020). http://godreports.com/2020/06/covid-silver-lining-pandemic-shuts-down-red-light-districts-in-india-sex-workers-liberated/.

Augustine. *Confessions*. Loeb Classical Library. Harvard: Harvard University Press. https://www.loebclassics.com/view/augustine-confessions/2014/pb_LCL026.3.xml?rskey=035QR0&result=2.

Bakare, Lanre. "Banksy Launches Homewares Shop in Dispute over Trademark." *The Guardian* (October 1, 2019). https://www.theguardian.com/artanddesign/2019/oct/01/banksy-launches-homewares-shop-in-dispute-over-trademark.

Bannister, Andy. *The Atheist Who Didn't Exist: Or: The Dreadful Consequences of Bad Arguments*. London: Lion Hudson, 2015.

Barnes, Anthony. "Who Killed Kenneth Williams?" *The Independent* (November 20, 2005). https://www.independent.co.uk/news/media/who-killed-kenneth-williams-516156.html.

Becker, Ernest. *The Denial of Death.* New York: Simon & Schuster, 1973.

———. *Escape from Evil.* New York: Free Press, 1975.

Bruce, F. F. *The Books and the Parchments: Some Chapters on the Transmission of the Bible.* 3rd and Revised ed. London: Pickering & Inglis, 1963.

Brueggemann, Walter. *The Message of the Psalms: A Theological Commentary.* Minneapolis: Augsburg, 1984.

Bursztynsky, Jessica. "Disney Says It Now Has 54.5 Million Disney+ Subscribers." *CNBC* (May 5, 2020). https://www.cnbc.com/2020/05/05/disney-reports-33point5-million-disney-plus-subscribers-at-end-of-q2.html.

Chapman, Graham, et al. *Monty Python's Flying Circus: Just the Words.* London: Methuen, 1989.

"Christmas Cards from Beyond the Grave." *The Daily Mail* (December 26, 2007), 30.

Clark, Daniel. *Dead or Alive? The Truth and Relevance of Jesus' Resurrection.* Nottingham, UK: Inter-Varsity, 2007.

Cline, Austin. "Too Many Gods, Too Many Religions?" *Learn Religions* (July 23, 2018). https://www.learnreligions.com/too-many-gods-too-many-religions-248240.

Collins, Francis. *The Language of God: A Scientist Presents Evidence for Belief.* London: Pocket, 2007.

Cromarty, Hannah. *Coronavirus: Support for Rough Sleepers (England).* London: House of Commons Library, 2021.

Davies, Mike. *Late Victorian Holocausts: El Niño, Famines and the Making of the Third World.* London: Verso, 2001.

Dawkins, Richard. *The God Delusion.* London: Black Swan, 2007.

———. *River Out of Eden: A Darwinian View of Life.* London: Wiedenfeld & Nicholson, 1995.

Dirckx, Sharon. *Why? Looking at God, Evil and Personal Suffering.* Nottingham, UK: Inter-Varsity, 2013.

Duffy, Bobby, and Daniel Allington. "Three Ways People Are Reacting to Coronavirus: 'Accepting', 'Suffering' and 'Resisting.'" *The Conversation* (April 29, 2020). https://theconversation.com/three-ways-people-are-reacting-to-coronavirus-accepting-suffering-and-resisting-137345.

"Ex-Lap Dancer Now 'Dances for God.'" *Christian Today* (April 3, 2009). https://www.christiantoday.com/article/exlap.dancer.now.dances.for.god/22982.htm.

Feinstein, Sharon. "Rock On, Freddie." https://www.sharonfeinstein.com/rock-on-freddie/.

Flew, Anthony, with R. Varghes. *There Is a God: How the World's Most Notorious Atheist Changed His Mind.* New York: HarperCollins, 2007.

Foltz, Richard. *Religions of the Silk Road: Premodern Patterns of Globalization.* 2nd ed. London: Palgrave Macmillan, 2010.

Bibliography

"'Food for Fuel: Olympian Phelps' Unusual Diet." *BBC* (August 15, 2008). http://news.bbc.co.uk/1/hi/world/asia-pacific/7562840.stm.

Frankl, Viktor. *Man's Search for Meaning: The Classic Tribute to Hope from the Holocaust*. London: Rider, 2004.

Gaita, Raymond. *A Common Humanity: Thinking about Love and Truth and Justice*. London: Routledge, 2000.

"George Best's 'Hours Are Numbered.'" *The Daily Mail* (November 24, 2005) https://www.dailymail.co.uk/news/article-369587/George-Bests-hours-numbered.html.

Gingerich, Owen. *God's Universe*. London: Belknap, 2006.

Harper, Kyle. *The Fate of Rome: Climate, Disease, and the End of an Empire*. Oxford: Princeton University Press, 2017.

Harris, Hugh. "In Defence of Viruses." *The Conversation* (April 22, 2020). https://theconversation.com/in-defence-of-viruses-136732.

Hedges, Chris. *War Is a Force That Gives Us Meaning*. New York: Public Affairs, 2002.

Hitchens, Christopher. *God Is Not Great: The Case against Religion*. London: Atlantic, 2007.

Holloway, John. *Change the World without Taking Power*. London: Pluto, 2005.

Hoyle, Fred. "The Universe: Past and Present Reflections." *Engineering and Science* (November 1981) 8–12.

ITV. "Life in Lockdown: The UK's 10 Most Googled Coronavirus Questions." *ITV* (April 2, 2020). https://www.itv.com/news/2020-04-02/life-on-the-inside-the-uks-10-most-googled-coronavirus-questions/.

Jobs, Steve. "'You've Got to Find What You Love,' Jobs says." *Stanford News* (June 14, 2005). https://news.stanford.edu/2005/06/14/jobs-061505/.

John Paul II. *Fides et Ratio*. *Vatican.va* (September 14, 1998). http://www.vatican.va/content/john-paul-ii/en/encyclicals/documents/hf_jp-ii_enc_14091998_fides-et-ratio.html.

Johnson, Sarah. "Coronavirus Survivor: 'I'm Still Asking Myself Why I'm Here and Others Aren't.'" *The Guardian* (April 9, 2020). https://www.theguardian.com/society/2020/apr/09/coronavirus-survivor-asking-myself-why-here-others-died-nhs.

Jones, Clay. "The Bibliographical Test Updated." *Christian Research Institute* (2013). https://www.equip.org/article/the-bibliographical-test-updated/.

Kellaway, Lucy. "A Point of View." *BBC Radio 4*, May 23, 2008. 10:00. https://www.bbc.co.uk/programmes/b00bcw2b.

Keller, Timothy. *Every Good Endeavour: Connecting Your Work to God's Work*. New York: Penguin Random House, 2016.

———. *The Reason for God: Belief in an Age of Scepticism*. London: Hodder & Stoughton, 2008.

King, Martin Luther, Jr. "Martin Luther King Jr. Speech." https://www.memphis.edu/libraries/mlk50/speech.php.

Kushner, Harold. "Preface." In *Man's Search for Meaning: The Classic Tribute to Hope from the Holocaust*, by Viktor Frankl, 7–10. London: Rider, 2004.

Larsen, Edward, and Larry Witham. "Scientists Are Still Keeping the Faith." *Nature* 386 (1997) 435–36.

Lee, Gracia. "Christians in Wuhan Emerge Boldly from Underground to Proclaim the Good News, While Giving Out Free Masks." *Salt & Light* (February 14, 2020). https://saltandlight.sg/news/christians-in-wuhan-emerge-boldly-from-underground-to-proclaim-the-good-news-while-giving-out-free-masks/.

Lennox, John. *Where Is God in a Coronavirus World?* Epsom, UK: Good Book, 2020.

Lewis, C. S. "Christian Apologetics." In *God in the Dock: Essays on Theology and Ethics*, edited by Walter Hooper, 89–103. Grand Rapids: Eerdmans, 1970.

———. "Learning in War-Time." In *Fern-Seed and Elephants; and Other Essays on Christianity*, edited by Walter Hooper, 26–38. 1939. Reprint, London: Fontana/Collins, 1975.

———. *Mere Christianity*. 1952. Reprint, London: Fontana/Collins, 1977.

———. *Surprised by Joy*. London: Fount, 1977.

Lewis, Geraint, and Luke Barnes. *A Fortunate Universe: Life in a Finely Tuned Cosmos*. Cambridge: Cambridge University Press, 2020.

Lloyd-Jones, Martyn. *I Am Not Ashamed*. London: Hodder & Stoughton, 1994.

Luscombe, Belinda. "'Having an Effective Vaccine by the End of This Calendar Year Is Achievable.' NIH's Francis Collins on the Big Push." *Time* (June 11, 2020). https://time.com/5842634/vaccine-nih-francis-collins/.

Luther, Martin. "Whether One May Flee from a Deadly Plague." In *Luther's Works, Vol. 43: Devotional Writings II*, edited by Jaroslav Jan Pelikan, et al., 43:119–38. 54 vols. Philadelphia: Fortress, 1999.

McGrath, Alister. *Surprised by Meaning: Science, Faith, and How We Make Sense of Things*. Louisville: Westminster John Knox, 2011.

Megoran, Nick. *Nationalism in Central Asia: A Biography of the Uzbekistan-Kyrgyzstan Boundary*. Pittsburgh: Pittsburgh University Press, 2017.

———. *Warlike Christians in an Age of Violence. The Evangelical Case against War and for Gospel Peace*. Eugene, OR: Cascade, 2017.

Middleton, Richard. *The Liberating Image: The* Imago Dei *in Genesis 1*. Grand Rapids: Brazos, 2005.

Milne, Bruce. *The Message of Heaven and Hell*. Bible Speaks Today. Leicester, UK: Inter-Varsity, 2002.

Murray, Ian. *David Martyn Lloyd-Jones: The Fight of Faith, 1939–1981*. Edinburgh: Banner of Truth, 1990.

Nettles, Tom. *Living by Revealed Truth: The Life and Pastoral Theology of Charles Haddon Spurgeon*. Fearn, UK: Mentor, 2013.

Noble, Holcomb B. "Dr. Viktor E. Frankl of Vienna, Psychiatrist of the Search for Meaning, Dies at 92." *New York Times* (September 4, 1997). https://www.nytimes.com/1997/09/04/world/dr-viktor-e-frankl-of-vienna-psychiatrist-of-the-search-for-meaning-dies-at-92.html.

Parker, Percy Livingstone, ed. *The Journal of John Wesley*. Chicago: Moody, 1974.

Perel, Esther. "Rethinking Infidelity . . . A Talk for Anyone Who Has Ever Loved." *Ted.com* (March 2015). 21:22. https://www.ted.com/talks/esther_perel_rethinking_infidelity_a_talk_for_anyone_who_has_ever_loved.

Perry, Flo. "Stephen Fry Says That if There Is a God He Must Be 'Utterly Evil.'" *BuzzFeed* (January 31, 2015). https://www.buzzfeed.com/floperry/stephen-fry-says-that-if-there-is-a-god-he-must-be-utterly-e.

Pisa, Nick. "Like a Prayer: The Italian Nun Who Spent 20 Years as a Lapdancer." *The Daily Mail* (April 3, 2009). https://www.dailymail.co.uk/news/article-1167112/The-Italian-nun-spent-20-years-lapdancer-shes-ballerina-Jesus.html.

Pollard, Peter. "Viruses Don't Deserve Their Bad Rap: They're the Unsung Heroes You Never See." *The Conversation* (October 29, 2015). https://theconversation.com/viruses-dont-deserve-their-bad-rap-theyre-the-unsung-heroes-you-never-see-46887.

Pontius the Deacon. "The Life and Passion of Cyprian, Bishop and Martyr." https://goctoronto.org/the-life-and-passion-of-cyprian-bishop-and-martyr/

Post, Kathryn. "NIH Chief Francis Collins Wins Templeton Prize." *Religion News Service* (May 20, 2020). https://religionnews.com/2020/05/20/francis-collins-nih-templeton-prize-winner-on-faith-and-coronavirus/.

Prothro, James. "Myths About Classical Literature: Responsibly Comparing the New Testament to Ancient Works." In *Myths and Mistakes in New Testament Textual Criticism*, edited by Elijah Hixson, Peter Gurry and Daniel Wallace, 70-89. Downers Grove, IL: InterVarsity Press, 2019.

Quarles, Francis. *Quarles' Emblems, Divine and Moral, Together with Hieroglyphics of the Life of Man*. London: Alex Hogg, 1778.

"Robben Island Prison Tour." https://artsandculture.google.com/exhibit/robben-island-prison-tour/mQIim-e6wopSJw.

Rosewell, Pamela. *The Five Silent Years of Corrie Ten Boom*. London: Hodder & Stoughton, 1986.

Russell, Bertrand. *The Autobiography of Bertrand Russell, 1914–1944*, Vol. 2. 3 vols. London: George Allen and Unwin, 1968.

Russell, Bertrand, and F. C. Copleston. "Transcript of the Russell/Copleston Debate." http://www.scandalon.co.uk/philosophy/cosmological_radio.htm.

Sartre, Jean-Paul. *Nausea*. Translated by Robert Baldick. London: Penguin, 2000.

———. *Words*. Translated by Irene Clephane. London: Penguin, 1964.

"The Science of Religion: Where Angels No Longer Fear to Tread." *The Economist* (March 22, 2008) 103–5. https://www.economist.com/science-and-technology/2008/03/19/where-angels-no-longer-fear-to-tread.

Seligman, Martin. "Learned Helplessness." *Annual Review of Medicine* 23 (1972) 407–12.

Sempangi, Kefa. *Reign of Terror, Reign of Love: A Firsthand Account of Life and Death in Amin's Uganda*. Tring, UK: Lion, 1979.

Bibliography

Shermer, Michael. "The Bottom Line for Me Is to Live Life to the Fullest." https://www.atheistrepublic.com/gallery/bottom-line-me-live-life-fullest.

Slack, Gordy. "The Atheist." *Salon* (April 30, 2005). https://www.salon.com/2005/04/30/dawkins/.

Smith, Laura. "Atheist Finds 'God' after 50 Years." *The Guardian* (December 11, 2004). https://www.theguardian.com/uk/2004/dec/11/religion.artsandhumanities.

Spurgeon, C. H. *The Treasury of David: Containing an Original Exposition of the Book of Psalms*. Volume 4. 6 vols. London: Marshall Brothers, 1869.

Tolkien, J. R. R. "Leaf: By Niggle." In *Tree and Leaf*, by J. R. R. Tolkien, 75–95. London: Allen and Unwin, 1964.

———. *The Return of the King: Being the Third Part of the Lord of the Rings*. London: Collins Modern Classics, 2001.

Tolstoy, Leo. "The Death of Ivan Ilyich." In *The Death of Ivan Ilyich and Other Stories. With an Introduction and Notes by Andrew Kahn*, edited by Andrew Kahn, translated by Nicolas Pasternak Slater, 155–209. Oxford: Oxford University Press, 2015.

Townend, Dan. "Last Days of Stalin: Soviet Tyrant's Doctors Too Terrified to Treat Him as He Lay Dying." *The Daily Express* (April 25, 2016). https://www.express.co.uk/news/history/663982/Last-days-Stalin-Soviet-tyrant-doctors-terrified-treat-lay-dying.

Tuan, Yi-Fu. *Who Am I? An Autobiography of Emotion, Mind, and Spirit*. Madison: University of Wisconsin Press, 1999.

Vonnegut, Kurt. *Breakfast of Champions*. New York: Delacorte, 1973.

Wallace, David Foster. *This Is Water: Some Thoughts, Delivered on a Significant Occasion, about Living a Compassionate Life*. London: Little, Brown, 2009.

Walls, Jerry, and Trent Dougherty. *Two Dozen (or so) Arguments for God: The Plantinga Project*. Oxford: Oxford University Press, 2018.

Ward, Brian. *Martin Luther King in Newcastle upon Tyne: The African American Freedom Struggle and Race Relations in the North East of England*. Newcastle upon Tyne: Tyne Bridge, 2017.

Waterson, Jim. "Choose a Better Future for All, Justin Welby Tells UK in Easter Sermon." *The Guardian* (April 4, 2021). https://www.theguardian.com/uk-news/2021/apr/04/justin-welby-uk-easter-sermon-covid.

Watson, David. *Fear No Evil*. London: Hodder & Stoughton, 1998.

Watson Institute, Brown University. "Costs of War Project." https://watson.brown.edu/costsofwar/.

Weir, Peter, dir. *The Truman Show*. Los Angeles: Paramount Pictures, 1998.

Wesley, John. *The Journal of John Wesley. With an Introduction by Hugh Price Hughes*. Edited by Percy Parker. Chicago: Moody, n.d.

Wood, Alex. "Andrew Lloyd Webber to Stream His Musicals Online for Free." *WhatsOnStage* (April 2, 2020). https://www.whatsonstage.com/london-theatre/news/andrew-lloyd-webber-stream-musicals-free-youtube_51313.html.

Lightning Source UK Ltd.
Milton Keynes UK
UKHW020815190722
406059UK00005B/119